POWER OF BIRTH PLACE

POWER OF BIRTH PLACE

S.K. Parashar

KALPAZ

ISBN : 978-93-5128-062-0

Price : ₹ 500

First Published 2015

Published by :

Kalpaz Publications
C-30, Satyawati Nagar,
Delhi-110052
Ph. : 9212142040
E-mail: kalpaz@hotmail.com

Laser Typesetting : Shubham Printers, Delhi
Printed at : G. Print Process, Delhi

Cataloging in Publication Data—DK
Courtesy: D.K. Agencies (P) Ltd.
<docinfo@dkagencies.com>

Parashar, S. K.
Power of birth place / by S.K. Parashar.
p. cm.
ISBN 9789351280620

1. Birthplaces—Philosophy. 2. Self-knowledge, Theory of. 3. Spirituality—Hinduism. 4. Parashar, S. K.—Birthplace. I. Title.

DDC 133.53 23

Power of Birth Place
is the brain child of
'Ek Dham'
(A spiritual place to attaining *moksha*)

Village or Post Office:
Bhatgaon, Distt-Sonepat, Haryana (India)
Contact No: 1091-8053788989,
09820258110
(residence)

E-mail: ekdhamindia@gmail.com

Organiser : Surendra Kumar Parashar

Date of beginning of this book :
11th March, 2011.

Date of finishing of this book :
11th December, 2013.

Contents

Main Points

1. Power and Importance of Birth-Place
2. How does the Birth of First Body take Place ?
3. How is the Pure Body ?
4. Search of Pure and Enlightened Body in itself.
5. Defence of Body by Soul E lement.
6. How is Brahma Matter. Virtue of Prakriti/Nature and Womb are Holding the Body or Jiva ? How does Body get free from them ?
7. Where is the Main abode of Jiva ?
8. How the Body Establishes its Empire on the Cycle of the Creation (Srishti-Chakra)
9. How is the Body of Four Eras or a Kalpa which Remain as God
10. How Long a Training is Required to be the Body a God of the "Kalpas"
11. A Body which Remains from the Beginning to the Final Destruction of the Universe. You can say it the God of the Kalpa i.e. Cognizant "Kalpeshwar"
12. How does this Body Remain Eternal!
13. How does it go from the Body to the Soul as Getting Enlightened from the Purified form and its Viceversa and who is the master of the able and the Ability ?
14. How does the Body get Aligned from the Body (Pinda) to the Substance (Anda) ?
15. How is the Supreme Body ?

16. How does the Linga Originate from the Body (pinda) or the Substance (Anda) ?
17. How does the Shiva Linga form and why to Offer Water ?
18. How the Shiva is Born, how it Becomes Shankar, How does it become Mahadeva and how does it become Mahakal or the giant man ? How is the "First Purusha" Swayambhu (Or the Supreme Soul) ?
19. How does Shiva takes Birth Ever ?
20. What is Supreme (virat) ? How is the Vishnu in the Supreme form ?
21. How the poison is Created ?
22. How does "Vishnu" Create the Atoms and how does he become Enormous by Devouring the Atoms ?
23. How the Shiva is Aligned with the Supreme Vishnu ?
24. Does this Universe is Prevalent Immersed in this Giant Vishnu?
25. How is Yoga done and How it Become Yogeshwar ?
26. In which Position Yoga Looks Incomplete to the Yogeshware
27. Does Physical Exercise Make Yoga ?
28. What is Difference between Yoga and Exercise ?
29. Yogeshwar of which Yoga or Asana Power ?
30. Is Vishnu Yogeshwar ?
31. How does Vishnu takes Birth Himself, i.e., birth of Vishnu?
32. How the Kal is Born ?
33. How do the Past, Present and Future Remain under the Time ?
34. How does Mahakal Overcome the Past, Future and the Present ?
35. Where do the Virat/Supreme Vishnu and Mahakal Live ?

36. How does the Prakriti (Nature) – Mahakal and Supreme Vishnu get free from the Dark ?
37. Is the Dark cause of the Death or the Death ?
38. How does one get the knowledge of Element from the Jal (Water), Agni (Fire), Akash (Sky), Prithvi (earth), and Air ?
39. How the Brahma or the Universe is Formed ?
40. How does the Narayana take Birth ?
41. Five-element Narayana i.e. how do the Pressure of Air on Water and Fire and the Brahma Light/jyoti Get Enlightened and Liberate the earth from the space, Prakriti (Nature), Supreme Vishnu Mahakal from the dark ? Is it the Brahma or the Birth of the Universe ?
42. Do the Brahma, Vishnu and Shiva Appear from the Narayana ?
43. Is Vishnu, Visha + Anu Combine Yoga to Yogeshwara Narayana ?
44. How is the Yoga and how is the Yogi and how is the Yogeshwar ?
45. Is the Existence of the Universe three. If it is, then how can be, if the Existence of the Universe is two, how it can be and if the Existence of the Universe is one, how it can be, If it is a Void, how it can be, how is the Indistinct or the Distinct ?
46. Is Prabrahma above the Brahma ?
47. What is the Declaration of the Prabrahma ?
48. Is the Alphabet Om is the Declaration of Prabrahma ?
49. Is Om all Supreme ? What is Om ?
50. How does it Want to have Supreme Feeling on the Noun, Name, Birth and Power/Existence ?
51. How the Brahma is Born ?

52. How the Vishnu is Born ?
53. How the Shiva is Born ?
54. How the Combination of Brahma, Vishnu and Shiva form the Yogeshwar Narayan ?
55. How does Yogeshwara Narayan Declare Prabrahma on the Alphabet Om ?
56. What is Om, tat, sat and what is Religion ?
57. Who lives in this Body named Devadat Satkam Named Purusha?
58. What is Karma and how it is Born ?
59. Why birth-death, profit, loss, Name and Fame are Born and What is their Secret, Wthe God has Kept them Hidden to Himself ?
60. How far this Body or Jiva can Reach after Achieving the Cognizance, Knowledge, Penance and Power ?
61. How the Sidtha Peetha is Made ?
62. How does the Jiva or the Body Decline ?
63. How Superstition is Born and how can be Saved from this Superstition ?
64. Why the Man Run Away from his/her Svadharma (Self Duties).
65. How far the Human Experience and Inference Reach ?
66. What is Sat-Asat, (Truth-false), Gyan-agyan (Knowledge-Ignorance), Conscious-unconscious, Distinct-Indistinct, Dark and Light's Position ?
67. How the First Purusha is made and how the First Woman of this Universe is Born.
68. How is the Creator of Shreeman and Shrimati ?
69. What is Adipurusha the Element-soul ?

70. How we will Reach upto the Supreme Element ?
71. How is the Person of a Strong Character ?
72. How is the characterless Person ?
73. How is the Unfortunate Person ?
74. How is the Religionless Person ?
75. How is the Wealthless Person ?
76. What is Remain/Shesha, Sheshanaga is the Emblem of which State ?
77. What is Special, is Supreme/Virat Special ?
78. What is Supreme ? If you meet the Supreme God, what will you say ?
79. Is Supreme a God ?
80. If to Meet with the Supreme God then...... ?
81. If you Meet the Giant God then what will Happen ?

Note : Main points are highlighted from book the text of the book so that readers could earily coimprebend and contemplate these points in the quest of getting answers possible. Readers each get answers of these points, if they go through the text of this book.

Is this book, body is not mortal. The proof of this is in this book. Till now this world has been saying this body is mortal. If reader wants to take answer of this, they can take from me.

Gratitudes

First and foremost I respect those aging people, women and youth of the village. Who donated strength in establishing and installing the statues of Shiva-Linga with Shiva-Family on 11th may, 2007 and on 20th may, 2007 in Shiva-procession. This Shiva family and the Shiva-Linga in this ancient Shiva-temple (Shivalaya), there is meeting with my tree (taru).

Afterwards I would pay my obligation obeisance to my parents who gave me this struggling body which is healthy till date. I pay my obeisance hundred times to them.

In writing this book, there are two persons. First person is Rishi Prakash Parashar who took ten pens in his hand and by giving me, he told me-take this pen and write history for village.

It is a relation which pressurised me repeated by and told to write a memorable book.

Expressing my gratitude I once again thank them.

S.K. Parashar

Introduction

Mother and the birth place is greater than the heaven. When this fact came in front of me, I decided- "Reality-in which home-family, society, philosophy of the birth-place, cognizance, knowledge, penance, power and renunciation, i.e., donations of property, rupees, paise and accounting one's own expenditure from others-the theme of the saying is that the philosophy of the birth place does not teach to seek help or good from others for the service of others is hot feasible. Even after reaching to some one's house do no accept food-cloth or water. It is meant to say that being dependent of one self by visiting the birth-place to be loved and give love to each and every particle of my birth-place and my birth. After wards my philosophy is feasible when I do complete expertion. Whaterver is with me I want to put them all on the stake.

In the process of passing the time the curiosity to decide whether this birth-place is greater than the heaven or not, made me constrasined. Hence I resided on my birth-place. Because I have been far away from my "birth-place" since my childhood.

Dear readers, what did I get or did not get from this birth-place. I am sharing my experience with you through this book.

Readers you are requested to give your suggestions after reading this book that what is the power of the birth-place ? This is my experience that it can get you meet to the god.

This is that power which shows the way from the "reality to the industriousness" and from industriousness to salvation, this is the soul power which get you reach from I to I or "me to me" salvation of the self. This is the same power which leads you to supereme abode (Param Dham) and Supreme abode (Param Dham) is the "abode of the God"-is also a pilgrimage, a place of worship."

Dear readers, me, S.K. Parashar by not writing to much, finishing the introduction and at the same time hope that it will give you a good message and you will like it. Second part of this book will also come named "your liking". The second part of this book will depend on your liking.

In this book, seven and half years of my life is contained. In this bivouace of seven and half years of my life I am finishing that in this book.

S.K. Parashar

"Power of Birth Place"

The curiosity to know the secret behind the birth and death leads to the path of knowledge aligned with the god at his door. Where the alphabet Om. Prabrahma, Paramatma (God), Yogeshwar, Narayana, the all superme is seated there. He is the ultimate place of worship (Dham).

"Ek Dham" (one place of worship) is the only path which tends to salvation.

In this treatise, the author considers himself an individual self, i.e., Dev (deity), Datt (ordained), Satya (truth) lustful body by keeping in mind the power of the birth place, which originated from Ek Dham (a place of worship). And this body would be a pious, pure and the enlightened body. How far we have impurified our body! A pious, pure and enlightened body how far can go!

The author with the chastity of this body how far he can walk......This is what the path tends to salvation or which goes to Ek Dham/or a place of worship.

Note : If the readers have a perusal of this book.....They can reach to "Ek Dham" – The place of worship. Please read it attentively.

1
Power of Birth Place

The Way to Salvation
Ek Dham (A Place of Worship)

This book is being written keeping is mind the all castes, society, community, creed and religion indigenous or Foreign, i.e., the whole universe.

I always hear from the mouth of a number of evangelicals and religious persons that control your desire, control your mind. O Brother! Desire is the art of the third number. The human body comprises sixteen arts. By preaching the desire or mind, these religious teachers fulfill their livelihood, bread, entertainment and licentiousness.

Do these religious propagators do not know that the body has to search other substitutes, besides, hunger and thirst. These religious teachers and propagators got privilege to preach from their mind. I am saying about those people, who are deceiving the people. I want to know that what is benefit of such thinking which has no alternative. Keep away such teaching from the meek people.

What is mind ?

What is thinking ?

What is the alternative of thinking and mind ?

These are the talks beyond the purified and enlightened body. First purify your home-family, society, village, city, birth and the birth place. Country will be purified automatically. If our country is pure, so how come the mind will remain impure.

In reality, only an industrious person can get the knowledge or path to search "ek Dham" (a religious place). Do in this present era such industrious people are there. Who can work for your home-family, society, village and the town.

If there is any industrious statue near by you, you consider that is your 'power of birth-place, pure and enlightened body'.

Such industrious body, in reality "ek Dham" or a religious place, wants to go towards salvation after understanding the importance of the power of birth place. Co-operate him in his search, that is why that body becomes power of your birth-place. Give importance to your power of birth-place and your insignia of your home-family, society, village and town to that industrious character, instead letting him fall because of jealousy, hatred. There are such people in this world who died in search of their birth and the power of their birth place.

A great warrior body found on account of the power of the birth-place and the birth. This pure and enlightened body becoming extremely charitable comes infront of the God. God ordained this body to be a Chakravarti king but this body refused this gift of the god because this body had dedicated its whole life in search of birth and the power of birth-place, which was also the great industriousness of this body. He kept searching the reality of the life. Do we understand it as the proof of its power and importance ?

This wandering pure and enlightened body gave importance to its character. The person who has lost his birth and the power of his birth-place, will obviously search for that definitely. If any thing is lost of a man in this present world, that person feels totally deviated and for that be ready to become characterless, dishonest, glib, greedy. Leave the talk of birth and the power of the birth-place.

How horrendous was the reality of this industrious warrior and on account of that he did not even ally with the god. Because this warrior was adamant on his virtue.

Can not this human house-holder society achieve the power from its pure and enlightened birth or the birth-place which can prove a great idol of a very strong character. We should try to do this.

Human being keeps working whole day and night out of his ego and he did not find that how far he has moved from his life.

When he has encounter with himself, he gets to have encounter with the "truth" also. So, take it-the 'truth' which is presented in front of you, to which you feel unable to say but only keep bearing.

2

A Naked Truth...... ?

You are travelling on an unknown path way, from a far distant place, you see a human form, ghost or a statue.

Does that human form or statue not let you feel that there is a Jivatma (a human soul) in front of you.

The power in between the talk or the statue or the form which vacillated from far away and the nearby-this feeling entrust you the truth behind the truth.

This is only an example which tends to the path of knowledge. When the human being goes beyond his acquaintance, he recognises himself. Hence, in this book there is the path to go from spirituality to the semi-god. This is the path to salvation: Ek Dham (a religious place).

Each and every individual has his aim permanently in this world. Whether they belong to one or this any other creed or community. Other species also choose their habitat in the nature.

There is a very peculiar construction in my body of which I consider my self a victim, although I am also like a normal human being I am from a noble family of high descent and represents the status of a middle class. However, a little bit literate who can understand I have interest in travelling right from my childhood. Perhaps,' life is blowing just like air blows, hence I am walking too.

I never had scarcity of opulence in this hectic life, for saying or feeling so, I have house-family but nothing happens in the home-family. Hence, I felt life just like an accident. It was a successful journey of life as yet.

Now I felt that the life is on the standstill or has been stopped, from here I am feeling a bivouac or break in the journey of my life.

A place is required to make a bivouac in the journey of life, at least grain, water is also required to live a life. Together with this, the idea had crept on religious, social and filial issues.

In last seven years, I expended lots of money. I emphasised excessively on the sacrifices, rituals, collection of offering of a great multi-tude (Prasada), Shiva-worship, penance, devotion. I have heard from the scholars:–cognizance, knowledge, penance (Tapa), power is found through sacrificies.

After experiencing this, I felt that I am searching a ray of light in the dark. The death of my elder brother made me constraint to move to the bivouac of spiritual penance. I felt my family is tending towards direction lessness. Keeping in mind the prevailing circumstances, I was fearing. If I also tend towards directionlessness in the process of walking on this path. In spite of being so conscious, sometimes I felt myself in the void. To get my consciousness, I would feel, where I am ?

Suddenly my attention would move to the conditions of my family. By the way, on the name of family I came to know.

Home-family is run through the sensitivity and possibility or love-devotion and not only through the wealth.

Generations of hard labour is required to make a nation but it does not take a minute to break.

I would like to say something, this type of man should be discarded from the home-family. The person who is very greedy and a great usurer, this type of person is a blot on the descent. Because, this type of person does not keep the home a residable home, he makes the home a shop and make the family a formal one. He can not cause to give medicine to the ill one. Because of this propensity the home scatters. It also happens because of family antagonism and the internal bond and in this bond someone may look his/her life in the family.

I think, somewhere this thought tended me to this bivouac. Where there is nothing in spite of having every thing. So why I am here ?

A place where there is no love in between the brothers and relatives, family members even a little bit, should be left instantly.

At this place-the paradise of the birth-place-there is neither grain nor water. The matter of the fact is that there is no respect for me.

Leave the grain or water, there is no place for bivouac at the birth-place.

This birth place was just like a bridleless more for me. I rode on this bridleless more with the power of my labour, wisdom, money-paise, renunciantion and the knowledge and succeeded in making a bivouac at my birth-place. How for the family or the home.....As far as my knowledge based on my experiences is concerned, I am not a married person. I am a gift of a real householder (Grihastha).

Now, it is another matter that I am getting opportunities to experience my industriousness on the bivouac of the journey of life.

The family headmen of every house is keeping himself alive on his door out of his resolve, though he is in an injured and illusioned condition just like Bhishma.

(Here the meaning of Bhishma is illiusion) He is a son or a grandson. He injures through his arrow and gives a new wound- This is the illusion of Bhishma's desired-death.

Floundering and living are the illusions of this family headman-Bhishma. The desire of this illusion keeps one self alive. On this expectation, any one from my family or descent, i.e., son or grandson give me nectar or the holy water of the Ganga (Gangajal).

Hence, he is lying wounded on the doorstep of every house by avoiding his world. This is the desire of illusion to live. But death is the final ending of this Bhishma or the illusion. Death is such a surprise which deludes the boon of desired death.

Now, how is this example for the Bhishma the family headman ? Lets see, how selfish he was, how far he can cause to fall the house-family.

At this bivouac, I saw a family headman, i.e., a Bhishma who was cutting the stem of the same tree just like Kalidas. He is trying to make his brothers weak and mendicant or because of his mean illusion letting them to reach to death. For him, his family members and his brothers did a lot, fulfilled his every wish, gave good upbringing, full freedom, service, marriage-even energy, family member co-operated him. But on account of his illusion, he scattered his family.

Althouth, no one was handicapped in this family to till date. This Bhishma, i.e., the family headman and his wife made the ensuing generation handicapped in its womb on account of their licentious averacious propensity. The youngest girl of this family is the witness.

How is this family headman or Bhishma or a disillusioned person who is only the slave of his facilities.

At the juncture of the bivouac, I thought to encounter the family head-man or the Bhishma ? Should I also put my every thing at the state. Because the power of the birth-place and the experience of home-family would be known for which I have made a bivouac.

Though, from the past seven years I have not spoken to this Bhishma or the family headman, in spite of this I was very much aware of his activities. Yes, sometimes a curiosity arose in my heart to make him understand but I thought-when his elder brother who had been observing sacrifices-penances, wished his well being by doing worship, is not ready to give him even three seconds, hence how will you make him understand, the person who is very similar to him will make him understand. Though this house was highly acclaimed in the village and society up to the last 30 years when he was living with his elder brothers. Now, this family is dwindling. This, the Bhishma of to-day keeps boasting of himself by gifting his family a heritage of a handicapped future.

Though, this Bhishma, the family head men, being a married one, I does not want to die like the Bhishma of the Mahabharata. His character is something else.

He is on the verge to finish his family. If a person like me tries to give him a very good suggestion, in the garb of dispelling him alleges bluntly and crosses all boundaries to cause him destroy.

In the guise of his averices and selfishness, he does not fear of even death to his near and dear one. Whatever he says and does in his family-home is considered right. Sufficiently he is the slave of his excessive usurious and greedy tendency. Enough to this, his another woman (wife)-keeps seeking her facilities through the allegation of theft on this deconsecrated family. His motive is only his freedom. There is no carefulness. Instead a family member from his house commits suicide because of his mean allegations.

Her thinking was so as that a beggar-mendicant has come to a high profile and well off family/house and says that this is not suitable for her. While her husband/Bhishma can not see anything except his wife.

A man like him whose tendency is so greedy and usurious can only be a blot on his descent. Though he looses his vigour but he never looses his egos. He remains very oblivion, though anyone dies in front of him without medicine.

Desiring to be the greatest and having vituperous languages on his lips, he never leaves his foolishness. Being the youngest he sought and got unwanted love which was abused by him.

The home-family having this type of family head or Bhishma looses its self-confidence and vigour who are dependent on him. For which it looses culture and his character also.

How a child of strong moral value can be born when the descent or home-family or the head of the family or Bhishma is like this.

By looking this character and handicapped future my mind feels baffled, suffocated.

Now, whether I will be able to understand the salvation (Parmartha) or not by anything from the cognizance or the empirical knowledge and being industrious, I do not know. Because I am incurring losses personally. It is noticeable if some one looses his accumulated capital. Career, the most precious seven years of his youth goes in vain. I have no complaint with my village, society and the family.

I have lots of relatives but they are only for saying so. Though there is mither expectation of grain not a meager drop of water. How this bivouac is! Because it is my subject that the power of the birth place is greater than the heaven or not.

This experience and knowledge will prove benefactor or boon for me.

I understand the importance and power of the birth-place, involved in my daily routine. I am seeing lots of changes in me.

My life went on changing on account of worship-recitations, penance and my religious propensities. Going to someone's house in the village or visiting home-family became a far distant talk, it was not possible to speak to any family member.

There was an useless place in a corner of the village to which I got that repaired after taking bath on the Shivalaya (or the Shiva-temple). This place has been under my mother's control from the last 40-50 years. At that place I kept doing plantation work and kept watering them and kept reciting Bhajans (religious songs) and worship.

At the bivouac of this time I was started to be seen just like a hermit and some people started to call me Baba too. (Baba-used for addressing the hermits/saints)

How do you feel if someone calls you Baba or a Sanyasin at your birth-place. Some on commented on me by calling hypocrite. Now at this bivouac I am feeling that there is no importance of relations.

As far as my remembrance/opinion is concerned, there is only a little need to combine the relations through your selfishness or remain in contact for others needs.

"Scholars are also of the opinion that kill yourself-I have no care of this, but I am alive because no one should feel remorse or sorrow because of my death".

One thing is proved from this opinion people are not able to break their relations with others they scatter into pieces themselves.

We keep living by making the name of the relations a shield. Is it life ? Yes, it is life, I do not want to live this crowded life, I do not want to do in such industrious work. I have to go beyond this industrious work. The bivouac of my industriousness is going to end.

Because the reason to live here has ended, the bivouac of the journey from reality to industriousness from 2007 to 2013 has also ended, now I want to go towards salvation.

Therefore, I have tried to get down those experience and knowledge which I have gained in the process of my journey from the reality to industriousness, from industriousness to salvation with my cognizance to understand the importance and power of my birth-place and heaven and the hell.

Now, by looking the circumstances of this place I have felt that I am here for someone's selfishness or someone else and I am not for anyone.

So, why these void 'words' have become a shield on the name of relations. It is better to tend towards salvation and think and visual is on eternity than thinking on the name of relations.

About that eternal truth from where people of the whole world comes out.

The path which leads to soul-element (Atmatva) to the absolute element. I thought this path can make me meet to myself. Achieving the absolute form of anything is the end of that thing itself. Its better for me to meet that person who is the owner of the absolute place of worship (Paramdham). This is the only path for me. The path which tends to salvations, the absolute place of worship (Paramdham) is the one and only one place of worship (Ek-Dham).

I am a writer. Collection of knowledge from different places has been part of my profession, i.e., To study the religious treatises or about the God (Paramdham) or garnering knowledge about the secret of life or birth-death etcetra, etcetra.

Talking about these things, one question arose in my life that the importance of birth-place is greater than the heaven. I thought, that I did not get to see the heaven. So, at least see which is greater than the heaven.

How strange was the talk of destiny, the time changed its course, a very strong incident occurred in life which led me to establish my bivouac at my birth-place, otherwise a very stupid would leave his career, and trade and settle in a village instead of settling in a metropolitan city. That foolish person is no one else, but that is me, my self.

If the train of life derails from the track once, it does not come on the track once again or if it come on the track. With great difficulty Sometimes, a fool like me has no place. Life becomes directionless and aimless. So the discourse birth-place in a distant matter.

So, I try to find myself again. Why I am here or where I am ? I start raising these question to myself.

Though, there is no downfall or any blot on my character. I neither remain in any filial, social or political matter nor I tried to participate in them. And my habit of pure vegetarianism, and the way of my dressing was so simple that I remained happy ensnared in that. Here I maintain my aloofness from the drunk people, habitual drug addicts or the ruffians wandering on the chowks or the fashionable stylish youth. If I encounter with them, I come out from there safely.

I heard about this village sometimes during my childhood. It is said that it was an ideal village. No, my age is not more than 50 years. After a long gap I came to this village or it was my long bivourac, only curiosity arose in my mind, saw some youth were standing out on the pathway talking. It seems they were well educated, perhaps they belonged to some well off family. I went to them and asked....what type of discourse is going on.

Reply : Now our mind got saturated in this village.

Why : What happened like that ?

Reply : Nothing else; every where violence, blood-shed, enmity-antagonism, denunciation of each other, treachery-theft, neither decorum to speak with the young or the old people nor the shyness is remaining.

Although, it is a very big village, people at least live here, it has been a historical village, brother!

Reply : In constraint, where to go, who has good quantity of their farm-land. Some people are accomplice in wandering and turned obnoxious by dint of unemployment, while some people are involved in their averices and show-off or have become victims of bad habit like smacks, liquor, licentious-this village is becoming a history of these type of people. So, these people have been detained and they are in the jails, even policemen wish good omen and wish let this village remain. They do not feel ashamed from their mother, sisters and daughters in such a historical village.

I was very astonished, he came and shouted on me vociferously. I asked a question in calm, getting an opportunity, he replied, no brother. It has been an ideal villagae. I used to hear this during my childhood.

Reply : enough, let you leave it (walking in irritation) were ideals still there aiming after listening this much. Live here some day and see, you will forget your own ideals. Go and do your work-otherwise we are going.

They went and I kept seeing them surprising and started thinking. It is a strange matter and how did this 700 year old village turn ?

The village which remained historical and ideal in between 700 years of subordination to which the former President of Russia termed it an ideal village of India, why did that village not remain ideal in 65 years of independence.

This question increased my curiosity-the facilities which have been provided by the government after independence....

During our time cycle was a big thing to be bought. Now a days every house has a motorcycle, here land is also very fertile. Development is every where like pucca road and lanes from the town to village, pucca buildings bank, post office, hospital, power house, facility of electricity and water, besides these, three government schools, in fact, all round development. There is no calm and composed life in spite of lots of facilities. Whatever the historical tales and ideals of religious ideals, all have finished. One idea came in my mind, because of independence and educational facilities these development took place. Although, I thought, there might be something on account of that this village is so big.

It came to my eye, a cowshed was established by 30-40 villages and is being run in which thousands of villager have joined. There are some old temples, Shivalayas, etc., are there. One very peculiar thing came to my ear that living here two and half days meant living hundred years at other places, i.e., its two and half day equals hundred years of other places. As a matter of beauty. It was given an example. A small canal used to flow to the lands for cultivation in between the village. Once upon a time this canal flowed underneath fifty two pillars this canal was built by Shershah Suri. There were fifty two streams and swimming on that gave the feeling of the heaven.

Despite having these all things why the youth of this village has this type of attitude. To know these all, I also decided to make my bivouac at this village. Although, because of my simplicity or societal conventions, i.e., not to be married or not to tie the nuptial knot had their reasons, on account of that I did not participate in home-family-relatives or social functions actively instead I had developed the habit of live in simplicity. Whatever money earned expended on the festivals like Holi-Diwali or on the marriage ceremonies and building of home. Thus, life went on like Ram came and Ram went. Neither in my house nor people from outside counted me and nor I had respect among the villagers. Hence, became habitual to tolerate the insult of the both outsiders and the family members. If some one cracked jokes or teased or abused me, I avoided by laughing at them silently.

But, the incident which happened this time made me constrained to be serious, now I have bivouac in this village where whole of the doors are closed for me. I have to search out a path from here. Because time-limit is not determined of this bivouac. Hence I have made a plan of five to seven years. Life has been extremely rigorous. I have the patience, now what to do in this village, this is the question ? I had read some where in the Vedas. Enough running took place. If Karma is done religiously so its salvation will be the Artha (opulence). So I decided renunciation, penance on the path of religion, Bhakti-yoga, sadhna (meditation), Shiva statue in the Shiva linga in the temple any thing shiva linga in the temple eny after I ate religious of ferings (prashada) every year, every day I worshipped four times, for the whole year (365 days) in all four directions. Watch equality in nature and the Jiva. Not to take half, not to take help of warm in clothes even in zero degree. This gives me knowledge of the effect of the natural seasons. This is the part of my penance.

The biggest problem is to do Bhakti or renounce in front of the people of the birth-place, because it is difficult ot be aloof from the people of the birth-place who teased you, use bituperatives, cracks jokes and to licentions life. Own respect, position and respect of the descent has to be taken care of, if a blot on the society, relatives or parents or respect would be hurled in the village. In comparison with the town, there is no facility to have even tap in the village. During Bhakti live or renunciation, there should be at least a facility to keep the body alive. Because conscious bhakti is necessitated to imbibe knowledge, Bhakti, penance and yoga and meditations. It is also pertinent to have healthy body to know the soul (Atma).

People go out side from their birth-place for their physical benefactors and beg but living in between your people and facing them as a monk, it makes you feel ashamed. People's comments/ humiliation because of that people come to my village too and beg. And take benefactors for the religious feasts, viz, grain, wealth and services provided by the people of this village play with their emotions. Our villagers also lag behind such dubious persons. Afterward, that obnoxious person gets privileges at public places or restings. At the same place that hypocrite starts exploiting the religious minded people or devoters from their grain and wealth. People in the village spoil their life with the addictions of liquor, smack and among these free licentious person. Obnoxious people, youth and children, organisers of such religious feasts (Bhandara) get in to the category of hermits. Villagers do not understand this and the plays of religious hypocracy goes on. Those persons, licentious persons, intoxicants who are aligned to the Baba (hypocrite saint), propagate his charisma that the Baba is an enlightened saint. This is just like a superstition.

With my renunciation, pencance and experience I want to give a message that beware of such hypocrites, religious feast organisers and psudo saints, that's why the future of the new generation of the society or village does not spoil. I want to recite such superstitious people.

Do these hypocrite red-yellow and saffron clad Babas who arc in the garb of saints beg, accumulate monkey in the name of religious feasts to the urban people and the villagers. Afterwards they make their abode at a public place of the village, after liquor, smacks to our villagers and play with the children, spoil the life of the youngsters. Hence it is very debilitating to be or sit like a meek dog at your birth place.

If they are involved in the my privacy, people of the birth-place will hurl shoes on them, then they will come to know what is hypocricy. These hypocrites keep changing their abode because of their disrespect and humiliation, but keep accumulation of the goods for their licentious activities.

I would like to give a message through my renunciation, penance and experience that beware of such hypocrite feast organisers and do not let the future of our child got spoiled. This birth-place is a part of bivouac of my life journey.

Now, nothing is known about this bivouac, it will remain or not, the plan/budget of seven years has ended.

It seems, I have lost myself and having feeling that I am in search of the Khuda (god). Where I am ? Am I just like that what I came seven years earlier! Let me see, where I am ? In this journey of life my palpitation and my breath are questioning me.

3
Microcosm or Giant

I am microcosm or giant

I am an experience or inference

I am or I am not

If I am, where I am

Yes sir, this is the question which keeps repeating that where I am ?

Perhaps, I came to search myself on this bivouac.

Seven years have spent till now, my search from 2007 to 2013 has not ended. I feel every moment that I am searching my pretension to live or my being. But I go far away from the reality as I reach near the target. Slowly-slowly conditions seems acceptable. It has become just like a habit, I feel every one for some moment like my family members, friends, relative, know-unknown people, but whenever I feel lonely, I start searching myself ?

That where I am ? The Vedas say that the importance of birth-place is greater than the heaven. These are the Vedic matters. Despite having these all, I want the birth-place. And even to-day there is nothing in my character that I lack something. I am totally spot-less. I gave several proofs of renunciation, penance, religion and the Karma/rituals at this bivouac of the birth-place. Kept one thing in my mind specially that no one could face any type of difficulty because of me. Therefore, I did not go at any door. I had one curiosity that I had forgotten that where I am ?

At least I should see the heaven given in the teachings of the Vedas. You give several proofs of renunciation-penance, religion, Karma (rituals) at your place, i.e., the birth-place, people of this place start searching the stigmas on seventh generations and keep you humiliating by their mean allegations. It is not easy work to face your own people eye-to-eye by doing religious rituals, renunciation, penance. As long as I did good work, people tried to humiliate and demean me.

How you think a little bit, on my birth-place, my own people start detesting my name, fame, success, renunciation, penance, religious rituals, in that case the place of birth is a distant matter, I even forgot myself that where I am ? Perhaps this historic example gives some direction. It is unfortunate that there is neither dearth of those persons like Vibhishana, Sugreeva or Duryodhana in the past nor in the present.

The killing of Bali with treachery with the accomplices such as Vibheeshana and Sugreeva imprinted a blot on the character of Ram.

Bali termed Ram infertile, coward and an impostor.

When the incarnated person, epitome of sacrifices has to face a difficult test by renouncing Luv-Kush and devoted wife Sita has to take Jal-Samadhi (immersion into the water) then what I am !

Bharat gave an example of a loving and devoted brother who worshipped the dust of his brother god but when Ram returned with Sugreev and Vibhishan to Ayodhya then....?

Bharat posed a gauntlet of war to Ram that this is not the convention of Ayodhya? By killing own brothers to be crowned.....there dust of elder brother's leg is worshipped. If Lord the greatest among human beings entered Ayodhya with brothers like Sugreeva and Vibheeshan then he will have to cross my dead body. Lord Ram sent back Sugreeva and Vibheeshan before entering Ayodhya and hugged Bharat.

This is the incident of tryst with Bharat or the meeting with Bharat mentioned in the Ramayan. I want to see my villager like Bharat and want to give this message that be an epitome of cognizance, knowledge, penance, power and renunciation. Do not antogonise and demean with each other.....Breaking the relations are very easy, but in making the relations it takes several generations.

As far as opinion my is concerned I found-culture, civilisation and consecration at this bivouac of the journey of life, there were used to keep like a heritage but to-day people have become insane in hunger of privileges and opulence. Cognizance, knowledge, penance or renunciation are only remaing as a word. Jealousy took birth, journey of life is becoming difficult. Education and cognizance has become only words.

On the journey of life hermit, Mahatma, saints and the incarnated people whom we call the god, they also hided their soul in some part of their body. As for example, on account of rigorous penance, Ravan had his life in his navel.

Among the incarnated gods Lord Srikrishna's life was in the lower part of his leg. The fear of life is always there due to being a living human being.

After becoming the king of the heaven Indra asked Brahmajee-Indra says:– Brahmadev, if I am in deep sleep, there is danger to my life and body because of being a bearer of the body. Hence, I want to live without the body.

Brahmaji blessed Indra to be visible/invisible or expressed-inexpressed but he did not impart the full knowledge of this art. Thus Indra became the king of the heaven. Indra also faced the danger of life in his life-journeys

The art of hiding the breath of life in any side of body was learned through cognizance, knowledge, penance, power and renunciation. Situation now a days is that every one has disappeared. By giving a warning any one can become a fortune teller.

In the era of twenty first century the great doctors-surgeon, or the scientists are involved in relief work for the safety of their breath/life, but to whom we say the 'Almighty' and he has become a mystery who has confined the all sciences in his single knowledge. "Jeeva and Prakriti" (life and nature) are also just like their nature. As for example, nature has combined infinite virtue like a secret under it. Just like that, the greatest among the living beings, i.e., the human beings are also trying to run away from the nature with the force of their power, cognizance, wisdom, knowledge, sacrifice.

But having infinite virtue and matter the Nature/Prakriti Succeeds and over powers, wisdom, cognizance, knowledge of the human being in finishing them.

Jeeva, viz., the human being dies before he understands the game of the nature. That's why birth and death do remain the most surprising phenomena.

As far as my opinion is concerned doctors/surgeons or the scientists have no alternative or source which can either make or save the life.

Although human beings keep doubting each-other, if they have doubt on the existence of God, what is wrong.

The world is replete with the history, men have punished the incarnated gods and their angels. This is the propensity of the human race. Renouncers and sacrificies are worshipped after their death as the idols of souls or at the cemeteries. Whenever the great soul is alive, he is never worshipped instead he is also examined. It has became a human habit to hide their virtue, demerits. The fool forgets that whatever virtue, demerits he is ordained, he has taken these all from the nature (Prakriti) right from his child hood to death.

The way human being is involved in cheating each other, the nature snatches every thing from the human race. This is the climate of "justice and injustice". Prakriti or the nature does not tolerate over their self to the same way just like a human being who does not tolerate another person with their interests, By dint of its ignorance, the human being is ensnared in the cycle of life and death. He examines others by hiding their sins. Whenever his examination takes place, he puts his relatives, and his near and dear one in a great difficulty.

Because of this ignorance and dissension people have divided the god

here, how strange someone has written or told......
human being was sold
remained like a rock without its forms.
If he got the form then be became the God!

The greatest and the most surprising among all the creation of the nature, human being forgets that the god has made a final surprise for them the death. In front of this surprise every knowledge goes away. When this great and cognizable human being is afraid from the death, they move towards their god and hypocrite religious teachers out of superstition.

I have seen some people evading from their religion and their god (conversion)

Because of superstition, fear of death and ignorance they start worshipping saints and prophets.

When they do not get peace and tranquility, they move wandering toward tantrics, filthy, sinners, deceivers who are running their shops every where. These tantrics, saints, filthy, hypocrite give them talishman, spot and thread etc.

Now the knowledge of this great human being falls on the legs, of these hypocrites and fraudulents.

These hypocrites, by giving spots, threads and talis man call those fearful persons on the occasions of the next festivals, i.e., Holi-Diwali or Eid, that's why they can extract money from them once again. These great and cognizable human beings are trapped in the hand of these deceivers.

That's why shop of these anti-social hypocrites keep going. On every festival the spots, threads talisman keep changing The question is that-Is this the punishment of the Karmas of man?

Yes sir, non-industrious human being considers his ignorance as his cognizance and boats himself as the great being.

The life of such cognitive person and the great human being becomes the scape goat of superstition.

I saw taking a married couple who were M.B.A.

-Why have you come here ?

Reply : This is the festival of Holi. We want to get changed the thread and the talisman.

- I asked, what is the disease ?

Reply : Jee/ sir for the birth of a male child tantric ji is treating.

- I asked-Do you trust him ?

Reply- sir/jee, people say, that's why we have come here.

- I asked-You belong to a well literate and affluent family.

- Yes sir, I am an M.B.A.

- In spite of that you came here to get spot, thread and talisman from this hypocrite and orthodox tantric.

Reply : What do you mean ?

-Big brother, you are not married to the spot, thread and talisman viz. you are married to a woman.

Reply : what do you mean to say ?

- Boy will be born from a woman and not from a thread. Spot or talisman. You get treatment from a good doctor and take care of your health.

Reply : Thanks for Advice !

By saying this he entered into the house of the tantric. I kept watching susprisingly.

In the modern day of to-day such literate people (cognizant or the ignorant to be said) are there who are the victims of superstitioin. How are the victims of superstition. How and who will emancipate them.

These types of orthodox/superstitious people start blaming their family by hiding their Karma that's why a hiatus is created in the family. Thus the relations dwindle. Because of their ignorance such people escape from their religion (Dhama) Karma (fuction) and the Artha (economy) and leave their families too.

Besides home and family, social values also start destroying.

Now they come in contact with the peers/saint-prophets escaping from their religion and gods and by leaving their families they reach to the Gurus and the hypocrite religious teachers. They do not get peace and transquility here also then they fall on the legs of the fraudulent tantrics, sinners, filthy, thus to create a great difficulty for not only their home-family but also their filial relatives.

Because of superstition and ignorance people's sin aggrandised and thus the situation become direction less.

Therefore, the people who violate the social values by leaving their home-family, parents, elders, relatives, their descent ends and they prove destroyer of their descent an account of their ignorance and sin. They get birth in insects or in mean jonies or inferior generations. Even god does not take such people in his tutelage.

4

The Quest for Sat-Sanatana

Therefore, in the quest of my word sat-santana (Truth eternal) and being a word as a body I also kept revolving the words and the bodies. Because being a human being life has to spend. When I did not find the exact meaning form/shape of my words-sat-santana (truth-eternal) then I got irritated and came out from the world of the words.

My trail was going on to come out, go out beyond the Brahma curiosity. This is just like action or it depends on experience or inference.

I will say it a cognizance or experience in the bivouac of the journey of my life, because an individual searches himself in the dark at the bivouac of his birth-place-where I was trapped or asked himself "where I am ?" this moment. If he find any ray of hope, he takes the help of that ray and search out his path.

Understanding religious path or the Absolute element of the God was a ray of hope for me. Whatever knowledge or experience I achieved from the ray, I am writing that.

In the regard of the birth place one thing implies not only on one but also on most of the people. Leaveing their birth-place, whenever people go like inside or outside the country, city or megacity or any other place and be they the highest officials, trader, minister or holding a big position or having big name, you belong to that place where you are born. The nomenclature which have been done at the time of your birth through enquiry the most suitable name on the basis of your zodiac sign to an astrologer or a pundit by your parents, there is of course a place for charity for that.

This name is written in schools, on the ration-cards or at the place of birth and death during childhood.

One peculiar thing is that at the birth place where you are born most of the people born at that place call you through a small name with more in affection but this is based on your complexion, face, attitude, the way of walking/wandering etc. As for example Rinki, Pinki, Tinku, Motu, Chootu, any eatable thing like bringle, cauliflower, related to flower, chanda (moon), suraj (sun), etc., from these names people call you. The matter of the fact is that people do not call with their real names even in respect also.

The proof of this is found even to-day. If some one teases you with your childhood name, fight begins. It can be a cause of jealousy. Some people always try to demean others who have got success, prestige, big name, respect etc. And the person who live in simplicity are branded as insane. They do not get tired in demeaning and detesting others. While the gentleman be come the victim of such propaganda and feeling constraint, they leave their birth-place. Own family members in the greed of their shares in property and land start dissecting him. Life becomes pathetic. Suffocation is felt. Therefore, a number of people leave their village or the birth-place and migrate to the cities.

I have become a professionn to achieve vote-bank for the sake of politics, seizure of land at different places, liquors, expenditure oal perpetration and the perpetrators, or murders etc. have reached to the villages. The matter of the fact is that the sacrifice for the country from the government or the society has ended. Here every one sees to each other as a dishonest person, humanism has died. Individual is running away from each other by be coming very selfish.

Oh, what is the sentence! This birth-place is greater than the heaven. It seems that the knowledge of birth place as a heaven has been felt at the bivouac.

As I was feeling happy to take birth greater I felt to complete the life, sin, jealous and antagonisms floundering has been overshadowing, relations are going to end. To live in such a birth-place heaven is not seen instead hell is seen. It seems people are counting their last breathe, how the life will spend further, people are feeling suffocated, people are not cool and calm, they are running away like insanes.

The birth-place to which I used to consider greater than the heaven, I came to know through my experience, knowledge that if the condition of the birth place is like this, what is the worse in the hell like towns. Where village, society, family, relatives and neighbours, your friends, etc., no one is there to ask you anything, whether you are doing good work or the bad one for your facilities, you run away like insane being free from the fear of your birth-place. This blind run is carrying the human being towards the hell of the town. I will say it a hell it is a blind run. Endlessness is the cause of the hell.

Making bivouac at my birth-place, I came to know or experience or achieve knowledge that this blind-run is not only here but also there. So, I, S.K. Parashar will not take part in this blind run which is endless also. I will make "Ek Dham" (a religious place where castes, creed, karma/rituals will not be different, there will not be jealousy, sin and people will find themselves running for the supreme Dham and this will be done by having interface to himself. viz, I want to enter into the house of the god and do not knock the door of the heaven of the birth-place or do not go to someone's door and go to only one door.

5
A House of God

Thinking this, the path which goes to this house, I am writing in this book.

If any reader has any difficulty or complaint, they can either write, contact or meet me.

I am presenting this book on behalf of my village or my birth-place, Bhatgaon, a house of god.

Power of Birth Place

Birth, name, karma, caste, society, community, sect, creed and the country keep breaking and destroying.

But there is no change in the eternity (Sanatana). No one can make it or break it. These are eternal truth.

Such eternal truth, eternal Purusha the great human being proclaiming for the Shiva from the Mahakal being ridden on the dark and enlightened creation-cycle and by giving importance to his birth and the power of birth-place always seated in the Shiva like conscious position. This is the first body of the Brahma or the universe.

Whatever I experience about this great Purusha body, will be found in this book. I am a bdoy in itself, viz, Dev, Datta, Sat, Kam Purusha named body.

I have no opulence, identity or respect. I have only body which is in search of an enlightenment.

From here dead or immortal the god who is standing out in between the soul force and the supreme soul, this reflection is making constraint to think.

As far as my opinion is concerned about God :-

Vishnu, viz . Visha + Anu (atom) = Poison and atom)

Shiva means cold, just like dead body is often match of the Shat karma.

Now, poison is filled in the Shiva, it becomes Shava (dead). Dead (body) or Shava becomes cold. Sometimes at the time of death, I have heard that the body becomes cold, there is no life in this.

Now, it is proved by this that, in this dead Shankar or Shiva Vishnu is Absolutely present or present in particles. To answer this question, neither doctor or surgeon nor the scientists have the answers.

When we say someone 'Mahakal' or the Shiva-Shankar, when the poison reaches upto the neck of the Shiva, he has been called the 'Neelkantha'! Therefore, Shivaratri is celebrated in the Hinduism. In the neck of Shankar, Vishnu is present in particles, i.e., in only particles/ atoms.

Here the greatness of Lord Vishnu is proved and the Shiva is considered as the symbol of bounteousness.

Because of direct proof, the nomenclature of the virat/ supreme goes to the Lord Vishnu.

Hence, whether the nature (Prakriti) or the Jeeva (body) having adopted giant form, supreme or whether Shiva is with the giant Mahakal or immersed in him, the condition is of the darkness.

Now, how can it be possible to emancipate this Jeeva (body) and the Mahakal in the Prakriti or the giant. Dark is the death.

Dark will enter in the light or the *vice-versa*, yes sir, this question is very much there in front of the giant Prakriti or the Jeeva or the Mahakal.

They do not have the answer of this question therefore, a new address/name is required.

This address/name can be "Narayan", i.e., Nava-water+Ayan means the source of power from where the date ends. To which we can term as Parabrahma.

The palpitation of dark or light is the Parabrahma, i.e., the Narayan.

This truth-untruth (Sat-Asat), conscious-unconscious-cognizance-ignorane, expressed-inexpressed, light and dark parabrahma, etc., are immersed in the Narayana. You can recite this one Namoh Narayan (ॐ नमोः नारायण) or Om Tat Sat. Eternity (Sanatana) is incomplete without "Om".

The birth of Brahmajyoti from the supreme Brahma which reflects the destruction of darkness and the emergence of the Supreme Mahakal proves birth for the body of the Shankar as a bounteous giant. It also reflects the virtues of the Prakriti on the basis of their virtue.

Thus, this world is immersed in the supreme form Vishnu, bounteous form Shiva and the enlightened form Brahma. These all are controlled by the yoga, maya power of Lord Narayana. Therefore, who does Bhakti (devotion), recite "Om Namoh Narayan" you can say it "Om tat sat".

Om is immersed in expressed-inexpressed, Sat-Asat (truth-untruth), conscious unconscious, cognizance ignorance just like glory or you can consider its appearance through Om, This is understandable for all scholars, meditators, hermits and the yogis.

The effects of recitation of Om depends on it experience on inference.

Om emanates from the navel from where the Brahma appears.

OM is the Proclamation.

OM is the feeling.

OM is the supreme.

OM is the dimension of the life, OM

OM is at the helm of the creation. OM!

Alphabet Parabrahma is the OM.

OM is the link between the Brahma and the Parabrahma.

The birth of the universe is with the grace of the rules of the creator with the proclamation of the OM.

Hence OM is the cause of creation and destruction. OM is prior to every name, word and offering of the Brahma. With the recitation of om, every recitation and offering is useless. This is the eternal truth.

6

OM Sri Ram Sarveshubhutshu

Universal or in every one. Hey, supreme lord OM, you have changed your formlessness into a possessed form and appears on the planet. I, S.K. Parashar, pay my obeisance to you-hundredth time.

Sanatan Purusha (eternal body) who is immersed in the Brahma, Shiva is always linked with him. I start my prayer to him from here and pay my obeisance to him hundredth time. I call him from my inner heart by saying this-Har Har Mahadeva......!

The path which crosses from the Brahma to the Parabrahma also crosses from the Mahadeva. Besides this, there is no path to go there.

This is an eternal/sanatana truth. Whether one is a very great recluse but without Shiva his every attempt of penance is incomplete. Or it can be said that Prabrahma is got to become Mahadeva. The first eternal body or the Santana Purusha always just like a Shiva or a cold dead body like dark, viz, a Shiva like conscious-unconscious being like a substance, this question is still remaining which can be understood with the substance (pinda) (dark or death).

How can Shiva or the dead (Shava) be conscious, kept in a particle (Anda) or in a substance. This is just like a creation. Similarly eternal body (Santana Purusha) Shiva or Shava (dead) Tatsat (eternal truth) is lying inside the particle (Anda) on the substance (Pinda), this needs just a proclamation.

This proclamation nara, i.e., water "ion" emanating from the navel to the rack and entering into particle (Anda) or the substance (Pinda) and its final immersion into Shiva or the Shava (dead), viz, to reach at tat sat (eternal truth) to be considered as a bounty/grace of the "Narayana".

The name of this proclamation is OM which directly clashes with the tat sat (eternal truth) or we can say that tat sat (eternal truth) immerses in the OM.

This proclamation is controlled by the yoga illusion (Maya) of Narayan which can be understood in this term/sense.

The proclamation of the Parabrahma alphabet "OM" emanates from Naration-or Narayan. Here "OM Namoh Narayan" is chanted.

Here alphabet OM combines with Parabrahma Tat sat. There it is called "OM Tat sat".

These scholars, meditators, yogis, recluse are involved to know this secret of birth-after birth that's why they could do their benediction through their interface with this eternal (Sanatana) pure Purusha Mahadeva or Mahakal, mighty, destroyer, Shiva or the cold Shava (dead).

Now, while on the one side, interface with this is considered benedictory. It is a subject for the devotees, whose curiosity is involved in this. This depends on the grace of the Shiva.

But, here problem is something else that the Shiva who is himself in the womb (Andkosha) just like a dead that eternal shiva has to come out from that womb to conquer dark or the death by becoming himself Shiva from Shava (dead). Shankar from the Shiva.

In the Hymn "Vishnu Sahasatranam" Shivas names are considered as the substitute of the lord Vishnu.

Here, it is proved that "Shiva" is resides just like a particle or substance or a dead body near the heart of the Supreme Vishnu.

Now, transformaing the formless into a possessed form, an abode is required for this eternal purush having eternal body to this Shiva or Mahadeva or the supreme Mahakal here. And transforming this here, is a grave difficulty.

Because the giant and the supreme body or the almighty is in the dark-the eternal Shiva is inside the womb or the substance.

Now, Narayana or the Nara+ion which is a "Lord (teja) proclamation" from the water or the nara and which can carry forward this womb or the substance (Anda or pinda), in that case a new incident will occur (Here the lord means the birth of the Agni/fire and the air).

With the passage of time that "Kal" (time) which has come up with the Anda or the pinda (Womb or substance) from where crossing from different conditions this Anda or Pinds (substance or the womb) in which the Shiva or the cold dead body lying is the birth of the previous time because of its passage.

Here "Time and the past tense/previous time" have been emerged as two new terms. From this alphabet 'OM Parabrahma Narayan' and bursting from the Anda or the Pinda (womb or the substance) the proclamation is going to be done into the water, fire and air. From this inert earth or Prakriti and the Brahma the enlightened conscious power (or the fire or Teja (magnificence) takes birth.

Thus, the Brahma appears with being enlightened, transforming himself from the formlessness into a possessed body.

As far as my thought is concerned this and a on the pinda (Womb or the substance) is made of "Panch Mahabhutas" (or five elements) and air and sky (indirect elements). And these all elements are entwined into one.

I consider the universe on this is may opinion. Because of enlightened Brahrna in the universe this conscious or unconscious body exists. Here present tense time is born. Consciousness is the present time because the direct interface with the giant is the proof of the present time.

The formless eternal sat (truth) the god (Paramatma) (Hence the word Paramatma is being used for the first time). Almighty alphabet OM Parabrahma, Narayana, Vishnu or Vish+Anu (poison+atom). Giant and because of being supreme (Rajoguna), Brahma-because of being enlightened-the Satoguna and like the dead body Mahakal, eternal Shiva-represent the Tamoguna and because of all these three gunas the future time/tense takes birth. And the Mahakal is established above these three times.

Thus, the triple virtues (trigunas), i.e., Ragoguna, Satoguna and the Tamoguna are born. Prakriti or the nature is the illusionary form of the triguna Paaramatma (or the almighty god). Hence-the paramatma runs this creation/nature through the Anda ro Pinda (woml or the substance) being aligned with the supreme alphabet OM Parabrahma, Narayan, from expressed inexpressed or from the bornless to the possessed form or creates the nature.

Among the Pancha Mahabhutas, i.e., the five elements water, earth and air are seen, hence they are expressed otherwise sky and the air are inexpressed. Thus, It is proved that this nature/creation is made of these panch Mahabhutas (five elements). But individualty they are different from this creation or the nature.

Paramatma, Alphabet OM and Parabrahma Narayana is the creator and the destroyer of this universe or the soul of this eternal truth/science of this present universe is itself all supreme.

I, S.K. Parashar pay my obeisance to this almighty Alphabet OM Parabrahma Narayana and pray him with my folded hand and with the bending head :–

Hey OM

Hey Paramatma (God)

Hey Jagadeeshwar

Hey Iswar

Hey Almighty Paramatma who have appeared from the formless into a possessed form. I pay my obeisance to you repeatedly.

OM Tat Sat

OM Srihari Sharanam

Here, bending the head or the soul/individual is the self-religion.

In this prayer, any other religion or community or caste has not been emphasised.

This is an universal prayer or an Ananya utmost devotion. Now this triguna Rajoguna, Satoguna and Tamoguna with it dominant nature, viz, Prakriti (Nature) and the past tense, present tense and the future tense, etc., are seating underneath the Mahakal just like the dead seating underneath the Mahakal the etemal cold Shiva. This play of Anda and the Pinda (particle or the substance) in going on under the composition of the creation.

When this proclamation and the magnificence, air with water and fire and sky clash with Anda and the Pinda (particle or the substance) Brahma Jyotirmaya appears or the Brahma gets enlightened. Or Brahma takes birth and appears which is called the universe. Here appearance of the magnificent gaint takes place.

Now, the creation of this nature is the result of the inert and the conscious or from the unconscious to conscious, viz, cognizance is born from the ignorance. This is the cause of the enlightened Brahma.

Now, under this Anda or the Pinda (Particle or Substance) eternal Shiva or Gyanendra Shiva is seating or cold wave like the dead body and because of the origin of these tense/times, the Mahakal becoming conscious or unconscious from inertia to the conscious stage is eating under this universe in great defense.

When there was dark, this eternal ever shiva Mahakal before Gyanendra Panch Mahabhutas like water, earth, fire, sky and air had sat as Supreme power defensively. Just like lying dead body. Now, he is also enlightened Brahmand or the universe within the Anda or the Pinda (particle or the substance).

More over, there is a reason to beget the propensity of the dominance of eternal Shiva Mahakal in this universe as from inexpressed to expressed in a Supreme form.

Hence, how come the expressed power over the rituals will segregate its dominance over the dominant expressed power ?

The segregation of this dominant form will be possible, if this question of the composition of the creation controls this inert element and the conscious power.

Now this inexpressed power will have to come into two streams for the benediction of this dominant form of the creation.

The first stream is inert form natural (Prakriti) element which has infinite virtues while the second stream is the eternal sat (truth) science or the power of the consciousness which can show the virtues of the nature which enlightens in the Brahma form.

These two in combination will prove a boon for the welfare of the dominant form.

Because of immortality of the soul have the eternal truth (sat) or the Absolute element science, the dominant form will have to be transparent from the eternal truth.

Here, for the sake of unconscious knowledge of the dominat form will have to be in the possessed form the incorporeal form being conscious in the Brahma or the universe.

On account of the enlightened form of Brahma, the Gyanendra being in the conscious position, considered defended in the Anda and the Pinda (Particle or the Substance). But the conscious power and the eternal power which is in the missscrosscopic form, i.e., Paramatma (the Absolute element), science the soul will have to work in its expressed form.

Hence, there will be the possibility of the dominant form.

For this, alphabet OM proclaiming Parabrahma Narayana as the Absolute element, the eternal truth which crosses water, fire, sky, air and the earth and by begetting the word (shabda), touch (sparsh), form (rupa), pleasure (rasa), fragrance (Gandha) and because of its magnificence and making conscious to the eternal Mahakal, the enlightened and giant Brahma from the inexpressed form into an expressed form and the Gyanendra power which is lying into the Anda or Pinda (Particle or substance) has to provide the conscious power. Subsequently this proclamation will go through the conscious being as Gyanendra which is based like a dead body, the eternal Shiva lying in the Anda or the Pinda (particle or the substance) will create a mental condition.

Here the mind takes birth because the state of mind is the mind (mana) on account of the Panch Mahabhutas, word (Shabda), touch (sparsh), beginning (Adi) and the Magnificence (Teja) the mind will deviate. After that the conscious power will make aware the internal feeling which will resurrect the Absolute element and thus the body will have the knowledge of the self.

Self consciousness is the birth, giver of wisdom. Hence the meditative state of Gyanendra eternal Shiva, Mahakal which is just like dead will break on account of the Self-knowledge. Thus the power of consciousness will also affect that from its power of awareness.

The Absolute element in its smallest partictlet form with its magnificence and proclamation will pass a great hindrance from all the direction for the great and giant universe. That's why the Gyanendra eternal Shiva aware from the supreme conscious power, deviated state of mind, intrinsic self knowledge, wisdom from the self knowledge and with the magnificent proclamation of the Absolute element all the directions will be hindered and this will give rise to ego.

Ego is the death/or the Mahakal when the smallest particle or the magnificence and the proclamation of the Absolute element is not known. Then the Gyanendra, eternal Shiva's meditative state breaks and all the directions get hindered then the ego takes birth.

Our sensory organs can see the infinite virtue of the Prakriti or the nature under this giant and expressed universe under the tutelage of this enlightened Brahma. But the wisdom has no eyes, so it can not see the both expressed and inexpressed forms of the nature thus this deviated mind creates ego."

Wisdom is lying in between the mind and the ego which is just like a woman. The self consciousness of the man is the feeling that he is a man.

Mind is the propounder of the creation which takes peculiar virtues from the nature and provides it to the wisdom. Wisdom is not able to understand all the virtues and the specificities of the nature Hence to maintains its supremency it controls the infinite virtues and the figures of thought into the hearth of the ego. Jeeva or being is the cause of birth and death. Thus, the cycle of creation in between the jeeva and the nature goes on.

ENTRY OF JEEVA IN THE CREATION AND PROPENSITY OF THE NATURE

Transformation of Jeeva (living being) from the Anda to Pinda (from particle to substance), alignment of the substance into the nature. And the magnificence and proclamation of the absolute element causes the birth of ego which ultimately hinders all the directions of the absolute element. So the Jeeva Gyanendra, Mahadeva, eternal Shiva, Mahakal kept thinking under the cold like dead lying in a seed form in the Anda (particle) and thinking over the magnificence and proclamation of the Absolute element forgets and prepares himself to accept the subordination of the wisdom or the women and forgets him self-consciousness. Wisdom, viz, the women could not understand the Gyanendra. So, pious, the Gyanendra eternal Shiva lying under the Anda (particle) into the cauldron of the ego where all the directions are closed. Subsequently the ten directions of the particle breaks into different directions. Here the birth of ten sensory organs and a mind take place from the ten directions. It is here, only the Rudra who perform rigorous dance (Tandava) in the universe rests whose name is Mahakal.

Here, Mahakal takes birth. Wisdom. Female form of Mahakali, viz, Mahashakti who forgets the Satvik virtues of the soul element of the eternal shiva and breaking the meditation of the Shiva puts him into the fire of the ego and combines him into the nature and thus binds the enlightened Brahma, thus proves boon for the creation cycle. To the same the eternal Shiva Sanatan Purusha transforming from the formless to the possessed form into the Brahma from Anda to the Pinda (from particle to the substance), from the soul element to the wisdom, from the wisdom to the ego from the ego to the ten hindered directions from ten directions to the mind by pondering over with the foresighted eyes with the curiosity to know the magnificence and the proclamation of the micro-scopoic Absolute element breaks into peaces and thus the Rudra Mahakal dances rigorously (Tandava). The few sencory organs emanate from the ten directions (Five knowledge grabbing sensory organs and five work related sensory organs) and the eleventh mind combines into one Rudra.

From this Tandava performing Rudra, Gyanendra emanates and from the Gyanendra the eternal Shiva Karmendra emanates Thus the Rudra emanates from his own meditation.

As long as the creation is remaining,. the Tandava of the Mahakal will continue. This Tandava of the Mahakal will continue. This eleventh Rudra will continue crying.

Here, the Jeeva keeps himself involved in his thinking, knowledge and Karma. The Jeeva trapped in the cycle of the creation and envolved in the virtues of the nature finds special merits.

And it is very difficult to come out from the cycle of the creation, once he is involved in the virtues of the nature. Now, the question arises here that which are the Virtues or the powers of the nature from which the Jeeva does not feel free, it is a noteworthy matter.

7

How this Nature is Made

A Jeeva or a man develops the curiosity to know the nature element on the way of his path to know in his mind. Hence in the process of moving towards his supreme Lord with his in depth thinking and complete awareness and depending his soul element from the wisdom with his heart or mind recite his natural element/Prakriti Tatva like this.

When the consciousness general power in the body, all the sensony organs activates, mind seeks self satisfaction from th[illegible] wisdom, viz, the woman but when he is not satisfied he [illegible] constrained to have an argument. This constra[illegible]nd makes the man ill and this illness makes the ma[illegible] silent. Hence in the silent posture how can a man argue.

Yes, in the state of silence he can argue or speak but in his internal soul. This is the final stage of a man's death, viz, the last bivouac of life and men can do nothing except pondering. All the sensory organs and the breath leave the body. So the pondering also ends. Thus the Jeeva or a man becomes victim of the life and death in this nature by his wisdom. He can not overcome the nature (Prakriti).

Life and death generates from the following elements : water, fire, earth, ether, air mind, wisdom and ego, word, touch (spars), form (rupe), Rasa (pleasure), fragrance (gandha), five sensory organs, eyes, ear, skin, three virtues, i.e., Rajoguna, Satoguna, Tamaguna, expressed and inexpressed.

This is noteworthy to point out here that Twenty-two elements makes a Pinda or a substace in the womb of the nature. So the in expressed power remains in the womb. This is twenty third element of the Shakti (Power/divinity)

The twenty-fourth element is the soul (Atma) or the soul element which can be termed as the science of the God or the theology. God is different from the nature because of it being all supreme. Therefore, this element can be termed as science, soul, supreme sprit/erement, soul-element or the Atma/soul. The twenty fifth element is extremely microscopic the supreme element/spirit which goes from micro to the inexpressed level. Here understand this with great attention. This is the birth of the nature or the Prakriti (Anda). This Anda (Prakriti) or the nascent phase of the nature can be termed as the twenty fifth element.

[illegible] this alphabet OM, th supreme lord, God, Narayan, [illegible] termed father of sciences because he creates this nature [illegible]wn in expressed and microscopio and illusory power (Ma[illegible]kti) which gives birth to the all knowledges or it can be understood in this sense that all sciences are intrinsically entwined in it or all sciences begin from here. This universal soul/Vishvatma, i.e., natural element from the substance to the particle and the twenty fifth element Brahma is well-mixed with the supreme God or the Parabrahma.

To know about this knowledge. One has to become Mahadeva-A great yogi or saint who overcomes the time or the past, present and the future and declares himself as Mahakal. Mahakal is the first eternal Purusha, an the eternal Shiva who looks after the cycle of the creation. He is considered here a yogi/ hermit because being a warrior in the creation of this universe he become a bounteous eternal Shiva. Subsequently, by pondering over his soul element intrinsically he did not get ensnared in the renunciation of his wisom or the nature.

As far as my experience is concerned the external Shiva, Gyanendra, at the time of going out, a female like the wisdom and because of appearance of the theosopthical element or the Brahma related elements and the ten directions and Karmendra (Gyanandra consists of sensory organs while Karmendra consists of five working elements) and the eleventh element mind. This is the eleventh Rudra.

I want to say here that Bhakti/devotion is the most important factor to be a yogi/hermit or the Mahadeva and the Mahadeva require conscious Bhakti. Which has proved a boon in the welfare of the creation. This is in account of eternal Shiva's or Mahadeva's satvik gunas or the satvik virtues or it has its proofs also.

Here, this is my firm conviction that to know about the absolute element it is pertinent to be a great yogi/Supreme or the Mahadeva for a sanyasi, saint, hermit, scholar or a meditator. After that is possible to reach to a House of God otherwise there is no other path.

As far as my opinion based on my cognizance or experience is concerned eternal Shiva transformed all Karmendra organs, virtues of the nature and the theosohhy into the Gyanendra (or th sensory organs) and did not allow it to be outgoing.

This is the art of immortality of the Mahadeva or you can understand this in the sense that the eternal Shiva Mahadeva has done all these for the sake of becoming immortal.

This secret is my own experience. If you feel any type of fault in it, me S.K. Parashar will apologise for that. Forgive me for this as my ignorance.

The art of immortality of the Mahadeva wants a dominant feeling which can be the proof of the both expressed and the inexpressed.

As for example :

In the expressed water, thirsty is inexpressed

In the expressed earth, grain is inexpressed

In the expressed other, word is inexpressed

In the expressed air, power is inexpressed

In the expressed mind, thought is inexpressed

In the expressed wisom, knowledge is inexpressed

In the expressed ego, ignorance is inexpressed

The dominant gist of the expressed and inexpressed has two types of proofs-direct and indirect.

On account of immortality of the dominant gist expressed is a proof itself but it also requires proof in the inexpressed.

As for example, seeing the presence of a woman in man is a direct proof. This art was taught by lord Vishnu to Shivji in the Mohini Darshan. The presence of inexpressed woman in the expressed form of the male by experiencing this, the dominant gist of the Shiva appeared in his Mohini form. This art of attraction (Mohini art) was learned by the lord Vishnu-the giant through the yogic power or meditative power from the magnificent and englightened Parabrahma-the supreme god. This Brahma form of luminosity of the woman has appeared from the fire. To burn or to luminate or to impart the knowledge is the personal dharma of the female.

Therefore, Shiva Mahadev becomes instable by his attraction to the fire form Agni. Thus he started burning in his carnal desire. He was not able ot establish the dominant gist on the inexpressed form while this inexpressed power which belongs to OM Parabrahma Narayana that is also the power of the supreme god otherwise no one else-this is the eternal truth. This is my knowledge or experience or inference perhaps. It will not be wrong to say that if the Shiva Mahakal could not establish his dominance over the Mohini form of the dominant gist, then.....?

This is a big defeat for Mahadev Mahakal or it can be the limit of the dominant gist. A great yogi (saint) is the proof of the expressed power over the Mahadeva Mahakal. Darkness or the ignorance is the inexpressed. This conscious power is well mixed up in the inexpressed power of the giant dark. Which is regulated by the Yoga of the Yogeshwara. Through this down, yogeshwara expresses himself in the enligntened form of the Brahma. Thus, the yogeshwara expresses himself in this inexpressed power like this......

OM sreepoornamidamh poornamida poornatpoorna mudchyat!

Poornasya Poornamadays Poorna Mevavashishyate

OM shantih shantih shantih !!

i.e. That supreme and almighty god is complete. If the complete is added with the complete the resultant will be the same and if the complete is subtracted from the couple. Nothing remains, this is the combination of the expressed and the inexpressed or both of them are a combination. The God Narayana is bearing under him this illusory Mohini form or the attracting form just like the expressed and the inexpressed powers,. As for example, whether it is the human soul of the cycle of the nature or the nature, both of them are enshrined in him or the god is present in the every particle of the nature/universe.

Its last beautiful example can be seen in the total surrender to him ending the dominant gist which proves a boon in the running of the creation cycle. And the fecundity and the ferocity are the two beautiful parts of the nature. It can be accepted by saying this..... I am a human being/man, you are Narayana, I am in you and you are in me. This is the dignity of devotion/surrender.

Now, the dignity of the dominant gist of the Mahadeva Mahakal faces a great jolt by looking at the Mohini form,

This is the effect of the Rajoguna of the Prakriti (nature). Mahadeva has become important by looking at the Mohini form of the inexpressed illusion.

The puranas mention one instance which substaintiates that the Mahadeva was boycotted by eighty-eight thousand saints by looking at the impatience of the Mahadeva on him Mohini form, because it was against the rule also immersed herself in the water. On account of this boycoctt. Mahadeva kept bearing this insult impatiently because all the saints were boy cotting him.

Because of this defection or the separation from the goddess Adishakti Bhagwati and the boycott of the saints he forgot the illusory Mohini form which was full of Rajoguna and accepted the Satvaguna in his inner heart and transformed it from inner heart to the inner soul from inner soul to the supreme soul and thus becoming himself as an eternal Shiva.

As far as my experience or knowledge is concerned-perhap the eternal Shiva renounces his Rajoguna, subsequently he entered into the Anda and Pinda form at the entry point of the womb of the creation, this is called Shiva linga by the people. This Satvik guna/virtue being more conscious became englightened and immersed in the parabrahmead or the supreme element or the Absolute element thus appearing himself as supreme lord or the Jyoti Linga. Therefore, it is called the Jyotirlinga too.

The great renunciation of the Rajoguna and immersing into the satvik guna/virtue and becoming the body-guard of the regulated creation the Mahadeva proved bounteous.

Without the desire of Shiva, the Rajoguna can not be overcome or no one can succeed in doing this.

On account of renunciation of Rajoguna, Satvik guna

generates the renunciation of Rajoguna from the Mohini form Satvik guna and generation of the dominant gist on the Mohini form begets the Tamsik guna/virtue of the Shiva Mahadeva, from these two virtues :

Deities are born from the Satvikguna

Demons are born from the Tamsikguna.

The existence of the Mahakal or the Mahadeva is because of this Tamsik guna. Now who is that not afraid of the Mahakal.

Now, the fear takes birth from the Mahakal, devotion from the fear and bhakti from the devotion begets.

To be safe from the anger of Mahakal the mortal world or the divine world and the demons/monsters all were aligned to the Shiva linga composed in the satvik posture.

Therefore, after pouring water and the Panchamrit, leaves and flowers intoxicants, etc., are offered to the Shiva linga. There is a customer of the coronation in the worship of the Shiva. Linga, I would say the worship of the linga proves also bounteous.

Hence, eternal Shiva Mahakal blesses both the deities and the demons happily and saves them on different time.

The teachers of the deities and the demones Brithaspati and Shukrachary I respectively propitiate the Mahadeva by their Shiva-Bhakti. Pleased with the intense devotion (Bhakti) of Angiras lord shiva blessed him to be the guru (teacher) of the divine world. The word guru (teachers) is synonymous with the guru Brihaspati even in the moral world. The meaning of Angiras was a person who has offered all the juice liquids of his body to the lord Shiva.

Ravan had offered only his neck. These are the great evidences of the Shiva-Bhakti/devotion Despite this, the dominant gist ensnared in the Tamogunea to establish their rule over the Rajoguna, the virtunous/Satoguni deities and the demons keep fighting in the great and the giant universe.

Both of them the deities and the demons commit same mistake which was committed by lord Shiva during his Mohini darshan to establish his dominance over the supreme gist. Hence he has to face lots of himilation by the saints and he felt indifferent from the divinity Bhagwati and took lots of pain himself.

This is the propensity of the deities and the demon-the representatives, after two gunas/virtues of the nature (Prakriti) Satoguna and the Tamoguna to over power the Rajoguna. Not a single Jeeva or creature in 84 lakh yonis/era, supersedes the virtues of he prakriti/nature. Being a satoguni Mahadeva became an eternal Shiva while the deities and the demons lacked the Satoguna, made lord Shiva their most reverred god.

The eternal shivg sometime personifies himself as Kal/time/ death, sometimes the god of death, i.e., Mahakal and some times as the great saint Mahadeva watch the games of change of the virtues/gunas of the nature/Prakriti.

But the Rajoguni yoga illusory Shakti Prakriti/nature enters in her regular way, otherwise her visit is not possible. The nature/ Prakriti never allows external interference in its empire, call though it be eh personinfication of the god, but it him perishable also, viz perishes his physical powers.

Yes, if the lord Mahadev eternal Shiva has to see the virtues of the nature and its game of change, he has to ally with the nature. If he does not ally with it he has to fight with this Mahakali being Mahakali.

Therefore, the alignment with the Mahakal and the Mahakali Adishakti Bhagawati happens to be just like a severely fought war.

It is just like a developed with who fights with enemy conditions of her husband as her own religion contrary to this, of an outsides stares at that developed wife without her desire, she opposes him vehemently. Hence, where Mahadeva Shiva is ensnared with the Satvik virtues of the same places mother Adi Shakti Bhagawati renounces her Rajoguni Maya (illusion) and becomes Satvik and worships him with great devotion.

There are 12 Jyotirlinga in the world out of which 11 Jyotirlinga in India while 12the Jyotirlinga Pashupatinath is in Nepal. These 12 Jyotirlingas are satvik and supreme. Whose satvik form is just like a girls first twelve years. She worshipped him with the flowers and the fruits and offered him water.

Note : A baby is considered as a Kanya up to her 12th year, from 13 to 18th she is considered a girl, from 18 of to 40 she is considered as a wife and after 40 becomes only a woman and remains so in different relations to her whole life. this is the period of a female's age is in accordance with the rules of the nature.

Hence, the Adishakti Bhagwati worshipped 12 years with great devotion to the nature, so being happy with this worship, Shiva also blessed her. Otherwise, a female becomes a girl in just 13 years because of her puberty. Thus, mother Bhagwati Adi Shakti Worshipped for her 100 births consecutively. To these 12 Jyotirlinga with her severepenance and thus she got the title of Maurdunage by Mahadeva himself. She could not achieve this satvik and blows position in her 108 births with her stubborness which she achieved in only her I birth with the Bhakti of 12 years. Therefore Shiva is called Bhola. Sometimes he gets pleased very early on his devotees and bless them.

Because of her stubborn propensity, the Rajoguni, Maya (illusion) personified herself as Rudrani to break the penance of the Mahadeva Shiva, hence the lord Mahakal turned Shiva wore a garland of human heads of 108 births, because this Mohini-rupa (Veloptuous form of the Rajoguna Mahadeva got irritated and renounces the Rajoguni virtue of the nature, The Shiva linga is enlight ened because of his anger. To pacify the anger of lord shiva, his devotee offer water and Panchamrit on his linga.

But Bhagwati is also not less powerful. When lord Shiva personified himself as the supreme lord and wanted to watch the virtues and the game of change of the nature (Prakriti), at that time Bhagawati came there and bears the Shiva linga into her womb. Thus, the Shiva and the Shakti assimilated with each-other which culminates in the birth of different yonis of the creation/universe. Thus the Rajoguni illusory Shakti propitiated lord Shiva though her worship, devotion a pious symbol of love and by aligning with him, she observed prayer.

Hey Mahadeva! You bless me or come into my varna (Colour). Thus Mahadeva Shiva looking at her pious devotion worship and upmost love, he accepted the prayer of Shakti and aligned with her. The varna/compleon present in the alignment of the Shiva and the Shakti because of this varna Shiva-Shankar personilties himself in this prakriti and see the changes. This is the triguni illusion of the nature-the great/giant which brought the greata saint and eternal Shiva, Mahadeva or the Mahakal into herself. Nowadays Bholeshankar reside on the Kailash Mountain of the nature. His devotees believe like this.

One question arises here, is this Supreme Vishnu or some one else and this triguni Maya (illusion) eternal Shiva/Purusta, Mahadeva, Sadashiva are in the Anda-pinda. (in particle on substance form) or are the in the form of atoms or are they the microscopic part of the birth and fecundity ? Are they so small that an ordinary people can not see them from his naked eye.

Is this atom present in the light or the dark, one they complete with either the poison or the nectar, one the mortal or immortal? What is there in these atom seither light or the dark ? But as or as my opinion is concerned the Vishnu-Visha+Anu, i.e., the atom of the poison, Are they the atoms of poison or the nectar is hidden in them! Nectar will have to be extracted from these atoms of poison, so the creation is possible. Is the creation not present to this date ? Is this creation present in the atoms of poison or immersed in that ? By understanding this, I can guess on infer on make a simple judgememt that this giant world which is made of these small atoms or immersed in the atoms of the prison, this creation is made of the poisonous atoms. There is empire of poison on this creation. Perhaps it is becoming infinite and here started disintergrating in clash with one another. Now the empire of these poisonous atomsiana started to be smaller or perhaps these atoms of poisons hour started to devour each other or to swallow the poisons of each other or to swallow the poisons of each other. Who will fight with these hungry and thirsty atoms, who will empower them and how will be the creator (Leeladhar) or this giant empire ? whatever he is, he will be called like that.

As far as my opinion is concerned, it will be smaller than the smallest and after becoming like a giant, it will be infinite. But all these will be based on the experience or the inference.

A warrier fighting with these hungry and thirsty poisonous atoms will immerse with him felt in the infinite sea/ocean which were inundated from his own sweat.

By the devouring of these atoms, indigo complexion/varna will emerge. Becoming magnificent this indigo will provide different colour of the five or the ocean imaging out from them.

This Magnificence, by pushing the fire of the indigo which is expressed from the inexperssed, thus he will be called the father of the wind. The proclamtation-which will occur from this Alphabet OM parabrahma Narayana Vishnu, that will be the father of this Brahma.

Now, the form of the magnificence of this indigo colour sky looks infinite. And this looks like the enlighty·ened Brahma because of this indigo coloured five or water and the effects of its magnificence. It destroys the dark. The creatioin of Anda from the atom, Pinda from the Anda by creating this, it is basically inexpressed.

By becoming Gyanendra from atom. Anda and Pinda the supreme appears. He creates this creation from these three virtues/ gunas.

Thus, saving from its own poisonous atoms and becoming the shell of the Anda (particle) in the nectar like Pinda, it is the father of the grain.

Note : As it is known from my experience/my penance or through my devotion. I S.K. Parashar who has devoted seven years of his life in a penance, after this to my birth-place. This is a very peculiar experience for me. You do not think it as a special V.I.P on an almighty-do not think it from the eyes of any religion or any sect, think and consider it as your own dharma/religion. It will prove bounteous fon the society. Country and the religion and give a great message to all. This is my expectation that by understanding this you will be happy which will be a befitting reply to the cynic and the antagonistic sects.

Message : The person who generates the poisonous atom/ particle himself, devours these particles himself. This has to be understood.

While on the other hand, the same atom, Anda is made which saves these atoms as a shell from thour poisonous atoms and subsequently the Pinda atom-nectar becomes the father of these atoms.

Those atoms which are poisonous among the almighty atoms/particles devours each other and this almighty atom becomes most devoted transforming into the nectar like grain and subsequently grain eats the grains. When he eats nectar-So why this feeling of religion, sect and cynicism ?

To save from this dissension this continued self-religion, will be helpful in recognising this eternal Purusha. Hence the human beings should demean his/her own self-consciousness.

I S.K. Parashar give this message to the all the religionists and social workers or the citizens of this country. Save your self-conscious eterned Purusha who is sitting within your self.

Therefore, after this message, I also tend to eternal truth, i.e., the Sanatana-Purusha where the giant Vishnu or someone else.....!

'Now, through the devouring of all the poisonous atoms or homogeneours form of all the atoms that Visha+Anu (poison + atom), viz, Vishnu or transforms into the giant Vishnu who is the lord of that triguni illusion (Maya) or became a giant from a microscopic atom which is also a secret. Likewise, before the birth and the death, viz, one who is sitting above the abode of birth and death, because of ending the darkness by generating the light and being above the both-dark and light, the atoms of poison above the shell of the Pinda, i.e., above the Anda and the Pinda and because of the generation of the nectar like grains in the shell of the poisonous Pinda but above from the both-poison and the nectar...... It can be understood in another sense that above the being of mortal and the important, despite being the foundation stone of the creation cycle but unattached from the creation and an account of being insnared in the Prakriti with soulful feeling that is above the Prakriti, creation cycle and the Jeeva himself.

Thus the virtue and the Panchbhootas or the five elements being separate from the water, fire, etc., is above the obscurantism, this alphabet OM Parabrahma Narayana transforming himself from the formless into a possessed form personifies himself in the form of the giant Vishnu, he is expressed or inexpressed through his own desire which is above the knowledge/inference or the experience of the human being-is just because of unknowingness. That is almighty personifies himself through his own despite being free from truth-untruth, knowledge-ignorance, conscious-unconscious, i.e., inert-conscious, expressed-inexpressed, experience once or the inference.

This is itself a selfless desertion, i.e., it is like that, whatever is seen in this world, is just like that. This nomenclature or name goes with this.....Like that, No fear, non-chanting (Ajapa), Abhoon:, unborn like that nomenclature can be made.

The body is the confluence of different alphabets, the OM Parabrahma Narayana being transparent kills the atoms or a devourer of the atom can be said, being the possessor of atoms or taking birth from the atom, being present in this creation cycle, Prakriti (nature) and the Jeeva but being absent from these all, how it has come out from the obsourantist elements and pearsonifies himself this giant Vishnu, this is just like a mystery. How this transparency can be understood or can it be understood by saying only infinite-infinite..... It is like that.

To know the cause of being like this the direct (Pratayaksha) will have to be proved.

The direct proof will also seek its nomenclature.

8
An Experience and Inference

To hit my target I did lots of preparations by my excessive renunciation, penance, study, worship, to know about god, reading religious treatises, yoga-meditation and thus following the path of the saints and experiencing those, I started thinking from the Brahma to the Parabrahma, alphabet Om, soul element to the Absolute element.

I thought that if I have to think, than why not to think about the whole universe instead of thinking about a place, a relation, an area or a region, yes, karma is done religiously hence the Artha (economy) is considered as Moksha (Salvation) Moksha (salvation) is a Dham (a religious place). I have seen a number of things like ocean, sky, snowy mountain, modern rivers, etc., subsequently my mind cause to this point and started reverberating. After wandering the whole world, the whole universe and the whole eternity I had no faith in truth-eternity from this universe, I was about to leave, at that time I faced the splash of my thoughts on my mind (whether I should go or not). This splash of thought and words (parents, brother-sister, relatives, etc., are the only words. I, because of being a literate person I went into the world of the words. On account of having linguistic knowledge word-power becomes excessive. And kept inferring the meaning of every word and behind the meaning of every word some form or body came out but I did not find the meaning on form of my words-sat-santana (Truth-eternal or eternal truth) Hence, to think about such words went away.

Now, once again here : whether there is any word and be the meaning its form or shape or body it natural to revolve around the words or the bodies because of their practicality. Because I am the only word. Ahm Brahmasmi (अहं ब्रह्मास्मि) : viz I am the Brahma!

Therefore, in the quest of my word sat-santana (Truth eternal) and being a word as a body I also kept revolving the words and the bodies. Because being a human being life has to spend. When I did not find the exact meaning form/shape of my words-sat-santana (truth-eternal) then I got irritated and came out from the world of the words.

My trail was going on to come out, go out beyond the Brahma curiosity. This is just like action or it depends on experience or inference.

I will say it a cognizance or experience in the bivouac of the journey of my life, because an individual searches himself in the dark at the bivouac of his birth-place-where I was trapped or asked himself "where I am ?" this moment. If he find any ray of hope, he takes the help of that ray and search out his path.

Understanding religious path or the Absolute element of the God was a ray of hope for me. Whatever knowledge or experience In the regard of the birth place one thing implies not only on one but also on most of the people. Leaveing their birth-place, whenever people go like inside or outside the country, city or megacity or any other place and be they the highest officials, trader, minister or holding a big position or having big name, you belong to that place where you are born. The nomenclature which have been done at the time of your birth through enquire them most suitable name on the basis of your zodiac sign to an astrologer or a pundit by your parents, there is of course a place for marity for that.

This name is written in schools, on the ration-cards or at the place of birth and death during childhood.

One peculiar thing is that at the birth place where you are born most of the people born at that place call you through a small name with more in affection but this is based on your complexion, face, attitude, the way of walking/wandering etc. As for example RInki, Pinki, Tinku, Motu, Chootu, any eatable thing like bringle, cauliflower, related to flower, chanda (moon), suraj (sun) etc. from these names people call you. The matter of the fact is that people do not call with their real names even in respect also.

The proof of this is found even to-day. If some one teases you with your childhood name, fight begins. It can be a cause of jealousy. Some people always try to demean others who have got success, prestige, big name, respect etc. And the person who live in simplicity are branded as insane. They do not get tired in demeaning and detesting others. While the gentleman be come the victim of such propaganda and feeling constraint, they leave their birth-place. Own family members in the greed of their shares in property and land start dissecting him. Life becomes pathetic. Suffocation is felt. Therefore, a number of people leave their village or the birth-place and migrate to the cities.

I have become a professionn to achieve vote-bank for the sake of politics, seizure of land at different places, liquors, expenditure oal perpetration and the perpetrators, or murders, etc., have reached to the villages. The matter of the fact is that the sacrifice for the country from the government or the society has ended. Here every one sees to each other as a dishonest person, humanism has died. Individual is running away from each other by be coming very selfish.

Oh, what is the sentence! This birth-place is greater than the heaven. It seems that the knowledge of birth place as a heaven has been felt at the bivouac.

As I was feeling happy to take birth greater I felt to complete the life, sin, jealousis and antagonisms floundering has been overshadowing, relations are going to end. To live in such a birth-place heaven is not seen instead hell is seen. It seems people are counting their last breathe, how the life will spend further, people are feeling suffocated, people are not cool and calm, they are running away like insanes.

The birth-place to which I used to consider greator than the heaven, I came to know through my experience, knowledge that if the condition of the birth place is like this, what is the bad in the hell like towns. Where village, society, family, relatives and neighbours, your friends, etc., no one is there to ask you anything, whether you are doing good work or the bad one for your facilities, you run away like insane being free from the fear of your birth-place. This blind run is carrying the human being towards the hell of the town. I will say it a hell it is a blind run. Endlessness is the cause of the hell.

Making bivouač at my birth-place, I came to know or experience or achieve knowledge that this blind-run is not only here but also there. So, I, S.K. Parashar will not take part in this blind run which is endless also. I will make "ek Dham" (a religious place where castes, creed, karma/rituals will not be different, there will not be jealousy, Sin and people will find themselves running for the supreme Dham and this will be done by having interface to himself. Viz, I want to enter into the house of the god and do not knock the door of the heaven of the birth-place or do not go to someone's door and go to only one door.

9

Ahm Brahma Asmi

(I am the Brahma)

Here, the word, I self is born. The vowel, which takes birth from the magnificent proclamation of the alphabet OM Parabrahma with the assimilation of body elements-that is the father of the word, viz, reforming/rectifying the possensed form, it proclaims in this proclamation the father of the word is hidden.

Note : I can say this experience or the Knowledge as "I am the Brahma!" I am the Brahma or I am the Brahma where the word, is bounteous for the rectification, the dominant gist appears.

Now, being transparent the Brahma took the nomenclature of I am the Brahma subsequently matching the words with this proclamation, the dominant gist appears.

Here the light comes out from the dark and its vice-versa which is the transparent part of them both. The giant meets with the enlightened Brahma or its vice-versa.....This dominant gist has taken an eminent form. Perhaps, for this another entity/ power has to be transparent or to take the birth.

Here the violet colour transforms into the white colour after its enlightenment viz violet/blue-light or violet light, white-light and white glittering will appear.

That who is born himself, he is the owner of himself. This presents the gist of the power.

Thus, the transparent body enlightens himself just like the almighty makes a proclamation of the Brahma....I am the Brahma (अहम् ब्रह्म अस्मि!)

By saying this only an individual gets bless and this world becomes giant like Shiva, Mahadeva and the enlightened Brahma like the almighty.

Thus, the Brahma who is born like this is said-it is this/we will say this or understand this.

Now, we can say that the eternal Shiva, Mahadeva Sanatana Purusha being an almighty has appeared as the Brahma.

I have explained it earlier it earlier that the creation which is made of Visha + Anu (poison + Atom), the dominant gist, assimilated soul, being an almighty the great here of the giant power Vishnu and the eternal Shiva, the almighty from the Anda and the Pinda eternal purusha Mahadeva, death/time, i.e., dark or the dark is the death.

Mahadeva, the eternal Shiva overcomes the death in the darkness. At the time of its appearance the almighty is determind to appear. It is to be understood in terms of the birth of the time. The almighty who has appeared is to be understood in terms of the past or understand that the almighty has appeared is the present and the time which is passing, understand it as a future. The person who becomes the almighty in all the three times/tenses, i.e., the past, present and the future is to be understood as Mahakal. This almighty which is immortal intermingles with the Absolute element. Almighty is the self-consciousness.

These are not easy. The absolute element, the immortal element, self-consciousness-these are not easy. Absolute element, immortal element, self-consciousness-it is like this the creation has to go beyond the atoms of the poison.

Afterwards the entry into the owner of this giant power is possible. Thus, the perishable body soul lessness 'I' by finishing or by forgetting it.....

That giant abode of Vishnu or Vishnu Dham that is the only place of god (Dham).

After entering into the house of God, this mortal and soulless body the 'I' ends here and assimilates into the alphabet "OM" the Parabrahma. Assimilation of this 'I' into the giant is the path which tends to salvation to which I. S.K. Parashar say a "house of god" or declaring it a house of god.....This can be recalled, I thought or recited like this :

Vishnu, Narayana, Krishna, Madhav, Madhusudhan, Hari, Nara Hari, Ram, Govind, Dadhich Bamanam

OM Shree Hari Sharanam!

Importance of the Brahma in the universe....Ahm

Brahma Asmi!

Brahma sat jagat Mithya!

Brahma is the truth, world is the illusion. I start to highlight a talk on these.....

Why it is like this!....?

If it is like this, so I should walk by seeing or understanding him, likewise, what is the distance between the Parabrahma and the Brahma being an eternal-Santana Purusha I want to see the Absolute element through the soul element.

How and from where this eternal truth comes in this Brahma. How it is possible to see or visit it ? Do these immerse in this nature and by considering the lie, cunning, deception, desire (sexual desire) and anger as their teacher and by not trusting the house of a house-holder or by not trusting the nature of the god and confining himself in a single and privileged house and keep an eye on the door....to know this, there is me and my wife at my house and the facilities earned from the deception and the fraudulence.

There are five gurus/teachers of a householder and without them the house can not run. These are sexual desire (Kama) anger (Krodha), greed (Lobha), liquior (Moda) and attachment (Moha) with their consent these house runs.

I am not a married person in this Brahma (Universe). I am a Brahmna by birth living just like a hermit. I have no teacher (Guru). I am the gift of this creation cycle. I want to be free myself from any type of addiction in this nature. I am ensnared in between the subjects of the Brahma, culture, civilization, decorum etc. I have got in my inheritance from my fore fathers.

They showed me the most important path-the philosophy to search/inquire at Truth or the eternal truth.

I have inherited this question from my parents "the path finding philosophy or the guidance" to inquire the sat or the eternal truth. Perhaps my parents did not achieve this. So, they inherited me this guidance to follow this path.

Now, I am not a house holder, the secret of birth and death is lying on the door of a house-holder. These world by duties can be looked after by the house-holder Jeeva. How is it, it can not be seen because a house-holder emgaged in the materialistic world can not ponder over the secrets of life and death. This is just because of their five teacher-sexual desire anger etc. Thus, they get their death in the cycle of the creation with their addiction to the material life instead of their addiction to the subjects related to the Brahma.

An individual who has got an opportune time for his/her cognition/self-consciousness, he/she looses that and falls in different yonis/eras/cycle of birth/this is the cause of birth and death.

But I will understand the secret of life and death at my door as a house-holder but with utmost care and search the path of sat-santana (path of eternal truth) of my parents or my forefathers from whom I have inherited them.

It is just like this.

How the Brahma is truth and the world is illusion ?

I am going to begin this by highlighting my parents/forefathers and my birth.

My parents or forefathers would have tried to find out or understand or bring in the direct light the eternal truth, perhaps they would have failed in that.

Perhaps by thinking that, they gave me this guidance.

10
Guidance of Eternal Truth

This is not just like that. They did not give me only the guidance, but also imparted me good education and I also perused well. I completed my education from the middle school level to Matric, B.A., M.A., L.L.B, and L.L.M. Thus, they gave me food education and guidance as well to find out the eternal truth. Besides this, they named me satya. Therefore, I am truth (sat).

Truth and justice are just like the two sides of a same coin. Now I have two important work, first to arrange the bread of two times for me to run the life and the facility to run it and secondry to find out the eternal truth taught by my forefathers. Therefore, I reached at the foot-step of the court with all my degrees and diploma.

Ten people were standing out on the foot-step of the count in my dress. They asked my identification. I told them in reply-sir/Jee Satya/truth.

They laughed at me vociferously and commented on the laughing-Satya/Truth....And here ? I asked them, why ? Truth is not here....

They, by cracking a joke of mine, said, if you want to search the truth, go to some other place or world and knock their door.

I introspected into the past, thought and understood that I am still very far away from the truth even after taking these degress and diploma with great labour.

An individual among them caught my collar angrily and chided me-idiot, you destroyed the whole capital of your life, what you did this ?

Setting free my collar from his hand I said, these degrees would have hindered my path, by tearing them, I cleaned my path.

- He asked, by incurring this loss, which path you have cleared, atleast tell me that.

I replied, the path of eternal truth which my parents or my forefathers showed me. Turning myself back, walked away.

They kept shouting. I kept on walking. This was the beginning of my search.

- The sound kept echoing, you will not find anything on this path. You will not get anything.

From were, I started my journey/garnering knowledge to the universe/Brahmand and finished my journey.

Only one bivouac was remaining in the journey of my knowledge and experience. The door of a house-holder because of my unmarried status.

I always considered this house-holder ensnared in the materialistic life, sexual desire and anger etc.

They have no time to know or understand the secret of life and death or to search the eternal truth or the Sat Sanatana.

I thought my forefathers might have ensnared in sexual desire (kam), anger on account of their house-holder status. Hence they did not find the eternal truth or the sat Sanatana.

By thinking this, I decided to search the secret of birth and death or the eternal truth through renunciation of my carnal desires- and anger, by arranging all the requirement of the house and arranging all the facilities for my wife as being a house-holder and establishing my bivouac at the front of my door After having the knowledge of this universe, cognition and experience, only this bivouac was remaining-Lets see, whether I should see this bivouac or not.

I kept thinking and garrisoned in my deep thought. When an individual is garrisoned in his thought, he should take care of his karma. By thinking this, I decided.....

After searching and traveling the whole world, whole universe, when I did not find the truth or the path to the eternal truth, I decided that I with sit at my home silent and search here the eternal truth.

I will try to search the eternal truth from each and every object of this house which I have collected useful or unuseful, and let not to cross any particle of the eternal truth from myself, my wife even the every breath.

The time kept passing, I accidentally came to know that my wife is pregnant.

Now, in this house, only one thing was now-my child. I tried a lot, that I should neither think nor see and talk, etc., about this baby.

But what did I do, I was constrained. My guidance to the path of the eternal truth had declared a war between me and my child.

Instantly one question arose in my mind-why ? why I should not go to him, after all I am his father, he is my blood. Why I should not ask-what does he want ? why do you want to come in this world ? what will you do. What will you be ? why do you not understand and you will not understand.

My wife was sitting in front of me, she started saying to me, as it means he is listening this talk.

I told my wife-bending toward her stomach, how it will not listen. I roared to the foetus in the womb.... listen..... whichever

I did not do for me to know this sat or the eternal truth, listen, I am a well qualified judge, I am satya having degree of a judge, a Satya who dispenses justice about birth and death, a Satya who had denised his life, property, whole existence in search of sat or the eternal truth, I do not know whether you will be able to prove this or not....Satya.....!

I do not know sat or the truth......?

Wife was about to speak......me......indicating me to be silent......? And indicating towards the foetus, if you can listen or understand, undertand. This is your illusion that you will do something new coming into this world, you will not be able to do this......?

Listen......! It may be possible that you may be a handicapped/impaired, it may be possible that you may be an insane or I think you will be born a complete man like me and be educated like me and you will not be able to understand the sat or the eternal truth inherited from your forefathers......!

Now I understood......you will not be pacified, you are obstinate, you shall come, just like me......(This is the birth of the word 'I') on account of my birth I came into entity as a hindrance in the path of your forefathers.

Today just like me, you came as a hindrance, you defeated me......?

You see towards me at present......I am a blunt person about to live 55-60 years or 100 years and present lie from my toe to head.

In future, a person like direct lie who will be able to live 50-60 years or 100 years viz a new life who has begot you and will pass away......just like them. My forefathers had begot me and subsequently passed away......!

I do not know, when this past, present and future will end

and do not know when that sat or the eternal truth will conceive. Who will know, who will see, that......How will be that's colour-form, how will be that's shape, how will be that's stategy to carry me a house of God by introducing me to the eternal truth, truth and the untruth. For this Shiva is a bounteous path.

Therefore, on account of transforming Shiva himself as Shakti. Shankar viz Varna emerged in the form of Shankar. He is seated on the Kailash mountain for the benediction of the creation.

Shiva, by renouncing the Brahma related matter and contracting his working organs, viz, he is in the meditative posture in his soul element.

Note : Some scholars are of the opinion that has been done by Shiva-Shankar for being himself immortal.

But, my cognition and experience tells that he overcome the death (Kal) in the giant darkness/absolute darkness by becoming himself eternal truth, i.e., Shiva, almighty, Mahadeva. Subsequently he became Mahakal by overcoming the past, future and the present. Now by overcoming the Rajoguni illusion he renounced the Rajoguna from this universe an finally being inherent in the Shivalinga he is seated in the Anda and the Pinda.

Which is worshipped as Jyotirlinga by the devotees in India. By surrendering herself the Rajoguni illusory power (Maya Shakti) and for the regulation of the creation and with respect and gist utmost love, Bhakti or devotion being happy this varna Shankar become Bhole.

The proof of this matter is present in the every female of India. How much a female be rich or the rajoguni, she surrenders herself in front of her male form husband.

Yoga in alligance with the illusory power are involved in the creation of the poisonous insects.

Being enlightened from the Anda and the Pinda, the almighty appears himself in the form of Jyotirlinga with the permission of the Brahma. From this, all the directions came into existence. How these directions contract being hindened in the Brahma. From these hindered 10 directions, 10 sensory organs havae come into existence. Out of which five are sensory organs while remaining five are working organs and the eleventh organ is the mind and that is the eleventh Rudra which is named as the Mahakal.

Eleventh Rudra, getting finished from their infinity, they reach to the Mahakal which begets the death.

Thus, the eternal Shiva-the satoguni and Mahakal the Tamoguni in these two form the Mahadeva born.

Yoga Maya Shakti or the power of (illusion) appears as Rudrani and fights with him. This war continued to 108 birth and subsequent By.....! The alliance with Shiva and Shakti only took place when she became a devotee of Shiva, when she became the devotee of Shiva with love, respect and Bhakti, other Shiva being a Mahakal had cut the neck on 108 times.

With the surrendered gist and prayer of Shakti Shiva transformed him into the varna Shankar. The matter of the fact is that the alliance with Shakti took place not because of the fight, instead it happened just because of Shakti's love, respect, total surrender and her devotion.

It seems Shiva Bhole appears instantly in front of his devotee who recalls him with intense devotion and surrender in indiscrimination with devotee's language, creed, caste and Karma etc. It seems......There is neither king nor a pauper......!

Everything expressed-inexpressed, sat-asat (truth-untruth), consciousness-unconsciousness cognition-ignorance, etc., be in there in there ordinary position.

Here, on account of alliance with Shiva and Shakti, several insect yonis (species) had been born in complete darkness which were born with the poisonous atoms after the creation of this universe by lord Vishnu.

Those insects which were born in consonance with the panch Mahabhootas, were all poisonous insacts which had not developed their working sensory organs. They can be called Andaj or incubative. The poisonous shell of this Anda and Pinda or the Anda was born from the Visha + Anu (poison+atom). The owner of the power which appeared with Vishnu's gist, that appeared with the women posture of the giant.

This creation land gathered up the giant, Maya Shakti (the power of illusion), eternal Shiva, Mahadeva and the Mahakal in the darkness.

Now, this creation being enlightened with the alphabet OM Parabrahma and removing the darkness is present in the Brahma form which leads to the cognition of the materials.

Knowledge comes from the Brahma. All the features/virtues of the Prakriti or the creation are known as the matter of the Brahma. Life is enshrined in these matters of the Brahma which takes birth and dies here being enshrined in the Brahma matters. This is the cause of birth and death.

11

The Domain of the Brahma

Now, in this creation/universe, the giant form of Vishnu is inherent in the grain and is intensely devoted, infinite while the eternal Shiva is in the meditative posture in the water just because of non-alignment of Mahakal. Eternal Purushu the supreme lord Rudra who has also personified himself as the Surya Narayana in the infinite sky. Therefore, he is present in the meditative posture in the both the water an the sky. The evidence of the fire element is not possible without the Surya Narayana.

You can say here OM Namoh Narayana. The enlightened Brahma has created the universe, Jeeva/living beings, the nature (Prakriti) etc. Thus, he proffers benediction to these all.

Thus, that almighty alphabet OM Parabrahma Narayana personifies himself in the Brahma form and appear also in the enlightened form and in this personification. He becomes the father of this creation or the universe. It can be understood in this sense that one who is the visionary of the vision that is the creator of the creation.

We can understand this here in this sense that the sight of a formless to a personified bod is only the eternal position/state. To this state or position, we would say it the form of the Satyuga era on the period/era of the truth. Because all these are a very common state for that almighty God.

From the darkness to the enlightened state. It seems that the whole creation is the almighty itself. This eternal truth/satya has appeared in the form of alphabet OM Parabrahma Narayana enlightened in the Brahma form. This is the Brahma Philosophy. That is the proclamation of a word, here in any of the Brahma state, the experience of a bivouac of a house-holder......a house-holder addicted with the dominant gist viz the owner of the house is constrained with his own untruthfulness and attached is ensnared in the hand of the lord of the death or Kal! Ahm Brahma Asmi!

The magnificence emannting from the proclamation of the alphabet OM, this vowel gives birth to the word 'I'(self), the dominant gist gives birth to the ego.

Brahma proves himself satoguna because of the fire of ego which appears in the enlightened form. Or the virtue of truth/ Satoguni is the father of the dominant gist.

The magnificence of the alphabet OM Parabrahma clashes with the Brahma and as a result the proclamation of fire enlightens and gives birth to the Tanamataras/resonance. These resonance proclaims like fire hence the first word-Brahma appears.

Here the possessed form of Brahma appears from the formlessness.

It is proved from this that the Brahma himself is the almighty. One thing is also proved here that the alphabet OM Para Brahma personified into the possessed form of the Brahma which substantiates him as the creator of the universe.

This Brahma word proclaims with the resonance and being enlightened the alphabet OM Parabrahma Narayana is seated with his magnificence and the Brahma is seated with the fire. Here, four padas of the Brahma takes birth.

Intermingling of OM Para Brahma and the Brahma

Now, the enlightend Surya Narayana who is present in this infinite universe. This is immersed with the Brahma and the Para Brahma alphabet OM Narayana's magnificence. This Narayana tradition is accepted every woman of the world whether she belongs to one religion, society, caste or the country and they do consider their male partner as husband taking inspiration from the Shiva and Shakti. The matter of the fact is that the consummation of the Shiva and Shakti is the beginning of this creation cycle.

In this present world besides the parents, girls, women or a female herself keep searching their grow just like Shakti. Whatever species present in the world are regulated by the consummation of the Shiva and Shakti.

Therefore, I, S.K. Parashar declare from my knowledge and experience:-"eternal Shiva, Mahadeva, eternal Purusha" always bless and proved himself benedictory for the whole world, country territory, religion, caste, society or sect in this Satoguni universe.

When all species take birth from the Shiva-Shakti in this universe, all of them will also immerse with the Mahakal after their death.

Therefore, it is proved that eternal Shiva Santana Purusha is not for a single country or a single relation but also he is ubiquitous for all species.

Some scholars are of the opinion that Shiva is the substitute of lord Vishnu. But here is another eternal truth.

12
Brahma Truth World Illusion

The Brahma is the Truth, world is the illusion. In the domain of the Brahma the knowledge and the Karma take birth on account of the subject-word while the Surya Narayana appears from the Parabrahma form......that is Ahm Brahmasmi, i.e., I am the Brahma. This is the first word. The birth of this word, I, is traced to the alphabet OM Para Brahma, which is resonant and enlightened the Brahma appears from the proclamation and magnificence or the word Brahma appeared. This is the earliest 'I' or the self otherwise every 'I' (self) is mortal.

This is the path which goes from the self to salvation. the which is mortal with the worldly pleasure that gets the worldly pleasure of self. This wordly pleasure is the cause of birth and death of the mortal self.

It is proved from this philosophy that the Brahma is infinite. If the Brahma is infinite hence the giant form Vishnu is also infinite. If Vishnu is infinite hence the eternal Shiva being an eternal is also infinite.

There are three inifities in this formlessness to the possessed form. On these infinities all three the Brahman, Vishnu and Shiva are the important.

These three infinities are regulated by the alphabet OM Para Brahma Narayana. This Narayana separates the domains of the Brahma, Vishnu and the Shiva. It is like this......

The word 'I'(self) Ahm Para Brahmasmi belongs to Brahma. The end of the infinity is the Brahma. It is proved from this that the Brahma is inifinite. It is proved that as the name of the mortal body or the I self word lives in the Brahma viz the mortal body, i.e., the jeeva ends and the word name or the 'I' (self) Ahm remains with the Brahma. It is proved that the Brahma is the truth and the world is the illusion.

The creator of the infinite atoms or getting created from devouring all the atoms, i.e., Vish (poison) + Anu (atoms) Vishnu who is the giant supreme Vishnu made from the small to the smallest and from the big to the biggest who appears from the atom or the particle, expressed/appeared in the different species, the eater of himself, nectar in the enlightened Brahma expressed in the graint form, the seed form of the infinite species-the creation and the giant Vishnu expressed in the nature and the Jeeva gives this proof. As for example, this body is grain. It is called grain, subseqaently it eats the grain and immerses in the grain. Thus, the Vishnu resides in the giant form/power is called Vaishno and gets the abode of Vishnu (or the Vishnu pada). Viz the giant Vishnu immersed with the Vishnu himself. These all are expressed in the Brahma. This giant Vishnu is called infinite.

Eternal truth-the atoms of the infinite souls or the giant form of the particle soul is known as the Vishnu.

Thus, the infinite power of the giant Vishnu separates. The Shiva is always in the meditative position in the Anda or the Pinda. Proof of this is found at the 12 Jyotirlinga Pinda which are very famous these days. In this Brahma, it is called Shiva linga. The knowledge of the self is the Shiva, water, fire, air, etc., are the five elements. This is also a magnificence and the proclamation. The clash of these elements or the touch of these elements is the creator of the mind. Viz the mind takes birth.

From this mind, the knowledge of the touching is felt and form this cognition, wisdom is born.

Panch Mahabhootas, i.e., water, fire, air, etc., are the progenitor of the five sensory organs or these panch Mahabhootas are born form the atoms. Atoms are the smallest particles just like inexpressed and they are the giant form of the Vishnu also. Giant is the ego. This is the birth of inert nature. This inert nature is inherent in the giant nature.

Thus, the eternal Shiva is also lying in his cognitive self. Here the cognition of the soul takes place thus, it becomes a dominant gist. It is meant to said that the Shiva is lying in the soul element. This is the state of the eternal Shiva. The deviated mind or the self cognition can push the wisdom towards the sensory organs.

Because wisdom is the female form which will tend to generate ego/proud and in the fire of ego/proud knowledge will burn. Ego is the form of the fire. Therefore, Shiva remains always conscious and Satvik (truthful) in the meditative position in the Anda and the Pinda. This is the benedictory form of the eternal Shiva.

Now, the eternal Shiva enters into the Brahma and immeres back in the Anda and the Pinda.

At the earliert Shiva appears as almighty in the form of Mahadeva the be eternal Purusha, the giant overpowered the death (kal) in the darkness subsequently he who comes Mahakal by establishing his victory over the past, future and the present and now the Brahma viz he renounces his Rajoguna by overpowering the Rajogunig Maya Shakit (illusory power) in this universe. Subsequently, Shiva linga in the form of Anda and the Pinda inherent in his meditative state.

Shiva is worshipped as 12 Jyotirlinga form by his devotees in India.

For the regulation of the creation the Rajoguni illusory power with great devotion, respect, love-adoration worshipped lord Shiva hence he transformed himself into Shankar Varna Bhole who is called Kailashpati in his personified/possessed form.

Thus, the separation of the eternal Shiva takes place from the formlessness state into the possessed form and he also separates from the ego and the demise/death. Among these three entities the material, nature have taken their place which are as follows :

The proclamation of the material, karma, cognition and the word, etc., from the mind is the illuminated and enlightened entity of the Brahma.

Wisdom is the male-female or the male and the female which gives birth to the death and the nectar and its instense love transform into the infinite dominance of the giant Vishnu. The cognition and the deviated wisdom, viz, forgetting the self cognition is the ego. And the power which finishes the ego/ proud is the entity of the Shiva.

Now, I think how to understand the entities of these three powers through the transparent alphabet OM Parabrahma Narayana. This is just like a trial for me. As for example, Nara, i.e., pani + Ayan (water + ion the magnificence about to come). Proclamation of the Para Brahma viz the universe or above the Brahma, alphabet OM viz the resonance of OM gets expressed from the inexpressed and hence becoming transparent.

Thus, the almighty God feels himself the soul element, material element and the conscious element while the science being expressed from the soul and the inexpressed absolute element alphabet OM Para Brahma Narayana separates himself. It is like that.

Brahma and the Para Brahma alphabet OM is the Narayana. You can recite it OM Namoh Narayana or the OM Tat sat.

Now the Brahma being enlightened, provides the creation cycle for the nature and the jeeva to involve theirselves in the fertility-fecundity activity, the giant Vishnu, intensely devoted and the infinite giving birth to the inert and the conscious species and personifying himself in the Vihsvarupa form or the universal form, being seated like Shiva or the dead in the Anda and the Pinda, devouring the microscopic atoms poison + atoms and bearing the microscopic form the Narayana viz Nara + water ions, from the magnificence to importance from importance to expressed and inexpressed viz the possessed form to the formlessness and making you feel the self cognition or seeing the soul, elementless, the absolute element himself/itself being inexpressed from the importance the alphabet OM Para Brahma Narayana separates himself.

Thus, the separation keeps taking place from the expressed to the inexpressed, from the inexpressed to expressed from Sat (truth) to the untruth (Asat). From dark to light, from conscious to unconscious, from cognition to incognition, from abstract to material and from the material to the conscious.

Now, one thing is proved here that the alphabet OM Para Brahma Narayana being separate from the nature is bearing Yoga in this universe.

Here we shall have to know the Yoga and the power of Yoga.

13
What is this Yoga

Now that alphabet OM Para Brahma Narayana is bearing this universe and the nature and in search of answer of this question eras have been spending. But, people keep giving their fact in accordance with their knowledge imbibed from the Upanishads, the Vedas and the Puranas.

All the scholars who have born to till date have given the philosophical discourses.

Showing the different organs of body in a somersaulting position or being seated in the meditative posture on an ashana, ending himself, it is meant to be said that the imagination of the body and the philosophy or form the composition to the Yoga try to substantiate them. The Puranas, the Upanishads and the Vedas all three have reached to the same conclusion in front of the Yoga since centuries with their raised hands. By saying three times......!

Infinite-infinite-infinite yadi Neti-Neti-Neti ! And at last with the Brahma or the universe the nature is immersed. In this age the treatise Sri Madabhagawat is being popularised which was written by Veda Vyas. Its first popularisation was done by Sukradeva. This treatise is just like a prayer. As for example......

Astoma sada gamaya-carry me from Asat (untruth) to Sat (truth) Tamso ma Jyotirgamaya-carry me from the dark to light Mrityurma Amritam gamaya-carry me from the mortality to immortality.

Several examples of the change of the nature and its art incarnated art forms have been mentioned in the Srimada Bhagawata.

But a very peculiar thing is being created in this Brahma or the nature.

This Sri mada bhagawata is understood by a group of people, a religion or a sect.

But that Almighty, alphabet OM Para Brahma Narayana has become a curiosity to be understood or to be known by different religions, different books, different languages different living standard, different communities/sects or the society in this age. Every one has his/her own claim.

How did these religions, sects or societies emerge. It is a noteworthy matter.

Cynicism and the orthodox religious leaders have founded different religions, i.e., Hinduism, Islam, Christianity and Shikhism, etc., and different sects and the society instead of the principle of the Sanatana or the path of the eternal truth. Moveover, selling different books, i.e., Bible, Geeta, Quran, etc., like treatises in a single shop just like the wards of a father lives in different houses. It is also likewise that the infinite inert conscious Jeevas keep changing in different species in this nature (Prakriti). Likewise these religions, sects, societies, country keep making and breaking.

But that alphabet OM Para Brahma Narayana confines the whole universe or the Brahma under his Yoga and remains in a single gist. This is the eternal truth Sanatana.

Giving four gestures like a money and running a shop on the name of Patanjali Yoga Vidya peetha is not a Yoga, it is a hyporisy. The hypocrisy does not long last. This is a propaganda sometimes on the name of religion, sometimes on the name of religion on sometimes on the name of religion.

14

Om Para Brahma Narayana Yogeshwara

Although every religion, sect, etc., are included in the Yoga, Jesus Christ in the Christianity, prophet Hazarat Mohamad in the Islam, Guru Granth Sahib in the Sikhism, Ram and Krishna in the Hinduism etc. Incarnated personalities or the great souls tried to take active part in it (Yoga) and give preachings/teachings to their religious devotees. Which have been well described in the Bible, Geeta-Ramayana, Vedas-Upanishds, Puranas, Srimadabhagawad, Quran and other treatises. Besides these some other religions sects are emerging with their own tenets.

But the real creator of this universe is an alphabet OM Para Brahma Narayana the eternal truth Purusha named Yogeshewara. This is the eternal truth.

Narayana is bearing this Brahma or the universe and no one else. Sat (truth_) is eternal and Sanatana is the eternal truth.

Remaining religions are the branches of the Sanatana. This is the Yoga and the creator of it. He is who separate every Jeeva, the nature from the soul element and bearing all in the Yoga. Nothing is separate. The father of all the souls is that Paramatma (God).

Now, I discuss those great souls who are called god in each religion. How many efforts they have made of reach the yoga. Did he be able to reach that eternal truth Sanatans Purusha alphabet OM Para Brahma Narayana Yogeshwara god, or confined to one religion or a sect as a god or a religious teacher in this nature/Prakriti. The separation of any religion on a sect without combining with the eternal truth (Yoga) is not possible in this universe.

Therefore, the Almighty God Yogeshwara himself separates all the religions.

The Yoga or God is the combination of everything religion and non-religion in between the truth out the untruth in between the cognition and ignorance, dark and light, the progeny tor of the nectar from the dead, abstract from the material, inexpressed from the expressed. Hence that eternal truth or the Sanatana Purusha Narayana, Yogeshwara himself, is the absolute element of the soul and he soulessness, God is the combination of the Prakriti, Brahma and the nature. If the Karma is observed religiously/judiciously, it provide the material pleasure and that Yoga is the god.

15
Yoga the Salvation

Therefore, emanating from the universe and the nature/ Prakriti to the alphabet OM Parabrahma Narayana eternal truth/ Sanatana purusa which reaches to the eternal truth/Satya Yogeshwara God is possible.

But going beyond the state of Brahma and the Prakriti mean to achieve the most pious position (Parampada) for a Jeeva.

But which type of the Jeevas achieve the most pious position (Param pada)? How it is possible. To achieve this Parampada, the following type of the efforts can be made.

God ordained infinite virtues to the nature/Prakriti by binding it is the Yogasutva. All these Virtues are changeable on account of their inert nature and moreover they are pragmatic also. The nature/Prakriti bound in the Yogasutra can not utilise its infinite virtues because all the elements and virtues are inert in the matter of the universe.

These elements and virtues of the nature are given for the Jeeva and the human being is the greatest being among all the Jeevas. Wise people are the great people among the human beings. Hermit is also the great.

Great among the wise and hermits ......

Knower of the elements

Knower of the soul

Knower of the Brahma

Absolute Known is the greatest.

Such hermit and knower, philosophy, knowing of the self. Theosophy/Brahma gyan and the knowledge of the divine element (Param gyan) experiencing these all by yogi can reach to the house of the God who is the alphabet OM Para Brahma Narayana Yogeshwara eternal truth (Sat santana) Pursha Paramathma and only reaching at the house of the god one gets the Yoga of the Param pada.

A House of God

In the house of the god which is the giant nature is shown by the Brahma. Mind becomes the subject of the Brahma of the virtues of the nature leads to determination/resolution. By determining the subjects the Jeeva gets trapped. By determining the virtues of the nature at least once. The mind of the Jeeva has no alternative. The virtue of the nature and the subject of the Brahma keep the Jeeva trapped in the cycle of the creation. The jeeva being the part and percel of the fertility and fecundity keep revolving in the yonis/eras of the Prakriti/nature and the Brahma. Thus the domain of the Brahma sustains. After revolving in the infinite eras/yonis and knowing about the Karma, Dharma and Artha the Jeeva bears the body of a human being.

Bearing the body of a human being he (Jeeva) reaches to the Karma, Dharma, knowledge and Artha (economy) and subsequently he reaches experience and inference. Through this human body a person can taste the nectar of the self cognition or the knowledge of the self.

After bearing the human body and aligning with the Karma and Dharma and Artha, he gets salvation. Salvation is the Yoga. Thus, the body is the medium of salvation. Human body is perishable just like a physical construction. It is proved here that perishable is the cause of development.

Brahma Satya, Jagat Mithya (Brahma is the Truth, World is the Illusion)

Now, a question arises here that how and who is the master of the giant supreme power evolved from the mortal body. It is a matter of curiosity that I should know that giant entity.

This question can be answered through the medium of human body.

Here boy is immortal and evolution of body/Body development.

The master of this giant domain plays a game like this. Because both of them are in the power viz they remain in the perishable and the evolved. It means the master of this entity does not die even after dying, that is immortal eternal truth. How this infinite remains giant individualty in single Jeevas. That is l ike this.

Being free from the Brahma, he is inflexible, or can not be named. As for example being enlightened from the Brahma the giant infinite is only a Nama and Rupa (name and form) or a word which is above the Brahma viz the Para Brahma.

Like the resonance recitation of the OM, the word Brahma is recited through the alphabet OM.

Likewise, the proclamation of the Supreme alphabet OM become inexpressed after being expressed. Likewise the mortal becomes immortal. Likewise, creating the perishable body from the infinite species the giant and infinite body and seed viz develops into the Prakriti/nature from the inert + conscious body......That supreme Vish (poison) + Anu (Atoms) creates the atoms of poisons and subsequently destroys these atoms or by developing those atoms becomes the giant Vishnu. Therefore, that Vishnu is like that. He is supreme. It is like that......This body is grain, there are hundreds of thousands of insects or atoms in it. It becomes intense because of birth of its ward. As for example, from one seed infinite seeds grow.

Therefore, it eats the grain and is known as grain also and is known as Vaishno in the giant dowain of Vishnu and achieve the Vishnupada. It is proved in the nature that destruction is the father of evolution.

It is proved from this, that on accout of being Supreme Vishnu is important in both destruction and evolution viz he is the giver of infinite birth.

While the perishable Mahakal, the bounteous form of the eternal Shiva, Mahadeva Shankar is a bearer of a body. Being meditative like a dead body keep an eye on the creation, this eternal Shiva is the alternative of the Vishnu.

As taking birth from the perishable the evolved form giant Vishnu likewise the Mahakal comes out from the perished, just like that the eternal bounteous Shiva Mahadeva Shankar comes out from the benediction.

Here, on account of that dominant gist difference is created between Shiva and Vishnu. As for example eternal Shiva almighty first Sanatama Pursha Mahadeva is the Shankar. Addicted/ ensnared/ inherent in the nature and unattached Vishnu and being unborn he takes birth and incarnated by his birth, there is difference between the attached and unattached Anbhooh: Prakriti.

16

Eternal Shiva–the Almighty Supreme Vishnu–the Abhuh

The eternal Shiva replete with the virtues of the nature is the Almighty. The Vishnu because of being giant is addicted attached in this virtue less nature is the unattached Abhuh and element less.

Now, Abhuh giant Vishnu and the almighty eternal Shiva and the nature and Jeeva being in the dark state are enlightened with the word Brahma and alphabet OM with its three resoncances appears with its proclamation. Therefore, the Abhuh giant Vishnu, eternal Shiva, almighty, viz., the Prakriti (nature) and the Jeeva (living being) these all are enlightened Brahma and the, etc......viz the three alphabets Brahma, Vishnu and the Shiva, OM Para Brahma Narayana Yogeshwra, Sanatana Purusha Paramatma (god's) house is the only place of God or Ek Dham.

Every thing appear from the house of the God. This is the eternal truth.

Now, in spite of having the dominant gist in the triumvirant, i.e., Brahma, Vishnu and Shiva......Brahma and Para Brahma is the important.

Here, Jeeva viz Dev, Dutt, Satya, Kam, Purusha is garrisoned by the Brahma Vishaya which are virtues of the nature, i.e., word, touch, form (Rupa), Rasa (Pleasure), fragrance (Gandha) with the resonance of the alphabet OM Para Brahma-Brahma.

Now, one question arises here that who will be the first Dev, Dutt, Satya, Kam Purusha among the Brahma Vishnu and Shiva who are seated in a dominant gist once this tri lateral) virtuous Prakriti (Nature).

In this question, the master of the expressed power wants to give birth to the development in this mortal and giant Prakriti and the Brahma. This is just like a physical construction. Now for the birth of evolution in the perishable the Dev, Dutt, Satya, Kam Purusha takes birth.

Here Brahma is in the meditative state as being enlightened in the yoga. Shiva is in the meditative state as being knower of the sensory organs (Gyanendra) in the Anda (particle) and the Pinda (substance).

In this giant perishable Prakriti (Nature) the first Dev, Dutt, Satya, Kam Purusha only becomes the Mahadeva. He is the eternal Shiva seated in the meditative posture in the Anda (particle) and the Panda (substance).

This Mahadeva keeps dividing in the infinite bodies in this perishal giant Prakriti which is also garrisoned by the virtues of the Prakriti and the Brahma matters. These bodies keep dividing in the virtues of the nature. Thus, the Jeeva ensnared in the Rajoguna, Tamogauna and Satoguna bears the Dev, Dutt, Satya, Kam Purusha, Jeeva or the body is not able to go beyong the nature. Jeeva remains detained in the Prakriti and the matters of the Brahma.

The Prakriti and the matters of the Brahma Pushes the Jeeva to theirselves from his self consciousness. Jeeva keeps revolving in he infinite yonis being ensnared in the creation cycle.

The Mahadeva ensnared in the giant and dominant gist of the Prakriti and with the influence of the illusory power of the Rajoguna were forgetting his self consciousness and thus being detached from the Dev, Dutt, Sat, Kam purusha viz the matters related to me Brahma and the virtues of the Prakriti he was being trapped in the illusory power (Maya shakti) and the rajoguni Rudrani. At that time Mahadeva appeared of that the Prakriti and the Past, future and the present time hidden in the dark started trembling, hene the the Mahadeva personified himself as the Mahakal and kept killing the Rajoguni illusory Shakti (Maya Shakti) for 108 birth because of her terrible form and the Tandva.

Finally the Mahakal, transforming himself from the great human being to the Mahadeva renounced the rajoguna and the matter related with the Brahma, hence Lord Brahma appeared.

Appearing in front of Brahma, Mahadeva requested that I renounce these 11 Rupa also.

Hence lord Brahma spoke-hey Mahadeva! these 11 Rudras which have appeared, you are the first person to see them along the 10 directions. Therefore, this human species which have born in this universe or the nature with these 11 Rupa will see your terrific form of the Mahakal. You will get other species also. The Rajoguni illusory. Power (Maya shakti) will also propitiate you. The Shiva-Shakti will prove a blessing and benedictory for the creation cycle.

By predicting this blessing lord Brahma disappeared. But he led the Rajoguni of the Prakriti anger and speak her self consciousness. Subsequently Shiva confining his working organs and renouncing the Brahma related matters and concentrating his sensory organs in his self-consciousness and with the great determination the Shiva seated in a meditative posture forever.

The Prakriti became competent to run the creation cycle through its trains formation of its virtueous form the Mahadeva, the great soul the first eternal Purusha on the Satya Sanatana Purusha. Besides this, by providing the liberties to prouote the fertility and the fecundity became successful to un the cycle but she did not succedd in achieving the Mahadeva. This was the defeat of the Rajoguni illusory power (Maya Shakti) Rudrani. To solve this problem the illusory power (Maya Shakti) Shiva, who is in the meditative posture in the Anda and the Pinda (particle and the substance) which is called Shivalinga by the people subsequent by he left his vision open by bringing the creation in a conscious willingly/soulfully, likewise the Vishnu being special is seated on the Sheshanaga in the Abhooh forms this Yoga Maya vision of the Vishnu is with the Sheshange which is open in a particular form.

Therefore, the Vishnu is the Abhooh, unborn, inflexible/ unnamed seated in the Sheshanaga in a yogic posture and keeping avigil eye on the giant world being aloof from the Brahma. The eyes of the Shesha is also open for the special.

Now, the Abhooh is seated on the Sheshanaga in the Vishnu form. The Almigty being immersed in the Anda and the Pinda (particle and the substance) and because of its special vision named Nagarupa revolves around the Shivalinga.

If this Naga sleeps, its eyes are open viz sleeps with the open eyes.

17

Conscious Devotion : Bhakti

Therefore, the followers of the Hindu religion have beliefs in the Nagapuja/Naga worship and celebrate the festival of the Naga Panchmi. By considering the Naga as a deity, it is also considereders a symbol off the Pitri Paksha. To give the cestors a respectable position the couple of the Nagas and the Nagas are established. Pitra Paksha keeps the future generation aware that's why the civilisation, culture and decorum be maintained in the family and the society.

Yes, if the family and the society fall from their culture, civilisation and decorum, the ganas of the Pitripaksha make them aware by their hissing like snakes/Nagas. They always want the growth of the ancestry. If the people of a desceht/kula fall from their decorum, so the ganas of the Pitripaksha becomes dangerous and started finishing that descent.

It is also proved that the naga/ snake the symbol of instance devotion.

Therefore, by not writing excessively, it is proved the Vishnu + atoms are something. Special, hence Sheshanaga is the symbol of advareness or the intense devotion. That who is seated on the Shesha, that is Abhooh.

He remains conscious in between the able and the enjoyer/ consumer.

Here Shiva is the cause of being almighty. He forgot the limit of resolution and alternative from the Anda and Pinda and from the Proclamation of the alphabet OM Parabrahma with the appearance of the word Brahma. Hence his self consciousness broke. As a result of breaking his self-consciousness he got ensnared in the proclamation of the Brahma. The knowledge of the magnificence and proclamation of Brahma made Shiva able to come out from the Anda and Pind, subsequently this first Purusha was born from the resonance of the OM Para Brahma (i.e. word, touch, form, pleasure and fragrance) viz the Mahadeva appeared in the almighty form.

Now, just after entering into the Brahma the Mahadeva was garrisoned by the subjects of the Brahma and the Virtues of the Nature/Prakriti. Because Prakriti (nature) is the female from of the wisdom. Hence Mahadeva got detached from the Brahma elements. Thus, Mahadeva got involved in the process of fertility and Pecundity by getting determined by the female form of the wisdom, viz, ensnaring with the Rajoguna. Tamoguna and satoguna and the Rajoguni illusory power (Maya Shakti), thus, finally involving in the creation cycle. Which culminated in the birth of infinite species. These species started effecting the creation/ universe. Because the most poisonous species/Jeevas took birth in this creation.

Hence, the Brahma ordered Mahadeva to stop the creation of the poisonous universe. So, Mahadeva asked lord Brahma- why he did make this body.

Subsequently, Lord Brahma gave the universe to the Mahadeva and told him I give you these 11 Rudras and 11 Rudranis. Now you the meditative Shiva will be worshipped ever by this universe. By ordering this, lord Brahma disappeard. Because of this every species meets lord Shiva after their demise. Permission from lord Brahma lord Shiva was going to sit in the meditative posture. So the Rajoguni illusory power (Maya Shakti) asked Shiva not to go from the universe/Prakriti. Mahadeva did not obey the

Rajoguni Maya Shakti (illusory power) so antajonism created between them.

On account of this antagonism Mahadeva renounced the Rajoguni illusory power (Maya Shakti). Thus the Rajoguni Maya Shakti started interrupting the path of the lord Mahadeva by beaning the form of Rudrani.

Hence, Mahadeva adopted his terrific form, i.e., the Mahakal form and appeared. Subsequently the Rajoguni Maya Shakti kept appearing in front of Mahakal in different form and indifferent births and the Mahakal kept killing her and the Tandava (terrific form of dance) kept going on. Thus, the Rajoguna inherent in the illusory power ended or got pacified, but Mahakals Tandava went on which represents his terrific forms. Because of this Tandava the Brahmaloka trembled hence Brahmajee predicted celestially-Hey Mahadeva please stop this terrific Tandava of Mahakal. Now it has become the cause of destruction of this Prakriti/nature. This Deva, Dutt, Sat, Kam of Mahadeva's body you got to run this creation but because of the terrific Tandeva of the Mahakal, this creation is going to end. Now, you achieve your self-consciousness and from this Shiva wil get the benedictory form.

Hearing the celestial prediction of Brahmajee, Mahakal stopped that terrific tandava and renounced the Rajoguna of the nature. From this fire of the terrific anger Mahadeva achieved his self-consciousness after that the eternal Shiva entered from the Pinda to the Anda form. Therefore, Shiva came to be known as the eternal Shiva.

Thus, the illusory power (Maya Shakti) Rudrani which is rajoguni also saw the eternal Shiva in the Anda and Pinda form. So she prayed to Brahmajee. Hey Brahma! I can not live without the Mahadeva. Please tell me the way to meet him. So, Brahmajee told Rudrani-Shiva is not separate from the Shakti. Whenever

Shiva will appear in the Anda and the Pind a form, Shakti will live will him forever. My statement/prediction will be a truth in the future. As the Mahadeva's anger diminishes as th Shakti will be meeting her. After that Brahmajee disappeared.

Now, this rajoguni Maya Shakti Rudrani got also seated in meditative posture in the Anda and Pinda with the Shiva which is called Shivalinga. He started worshipping him with the offering of flowers, fruits, leaves, water besides Panchamrit. She kept worshipping him birth after-birth.

The tradition of offering of water on the Shiva linga is continuing even to day.

A great human being Mahadeva, Mahakal named Deva, Dutt, Satya, Kam Purusha is seated on this Shiva linga in the form of eternal Shiva which is the almighty also or who is not under any one.

Shiva is seated conscious in the benedictory form in accordance with the rules of the nature or the creation.

One question arises here also. This is under the enjoyment and the enjoyer or the Brahma and the Para Brahma.

Now, there are two virtues of this nature-Satoguna and the Tamoguna while he renounced the third Guna/virtue the Rajoguna because of anger.

It can understood here that the anger emanated from the five which carries towards the Rajoguna of the nature which is just like the female form of the wisdom. Thus, Jeeva, i.e., Deva Dutt, Sat, Kam Purusha and the enjoyer becomes the able.

Because of the magnificence and proclamation of that alphabet OM Para Brahma the mind got an alternative in the Anda and the Pinda. Hene the Jeeva, i.e., Deva, Dutt, Satya named Purusha emanating from the Anda and Pinda got ensnared in the virtues and matters of the nature and the Brahma respect lively.

Therefore, Shiva got ensnared in the virtues of the giant Prakriti and the matters of the Brahma and thus he became the Almighty. Likewise the first Dev, Dutt, Satya, Kam Purusha named great human being Mahadeva appeared in this universe.

Now if we see at the level of wisdom the wisdom of the Mahadeva is being dtached from the soul element because of their entry into the virtues of the nature and the matters related toe Brahma.

Satoguna is leaving Mahadeva. On account of attraction between the virtues of the nature and the matters related toe Brahma and the presence of the Tamsik wisdom, he is seated in the Tamoguna posture.

Now, the vision and the wisdom of the Mahadeva is lying on the power of the giant Prakriti and the Brahma. On account of the infinite virtues and the Rajoguni effects of the matter attraction is created. This attraction has created the domination just in the Mahadeva. In this dominant gist the wisdom, Rajoguni Mayashakti Rudrani got awakened and appeared.

Because of this dominant gist they clashed. This creation cycle appeared because of the intermingling of the Rudra form of the Mahadeva and Rudra form of the illusory power (Maya Shakti) Rudrani, the Jeevas of this creation are the glories of these 11 Rudras and Rudris which have developed in the infinite species.

Being giant Vishnu is element less, unborn, inflexible/or not to be named Abhooh or we can say him "it is like this" which can be seen in the every universe. Vishnu bears every thing and everything is inherent in Vishnu which are before the inception and after the inception of the virtues and Karma of the Prakriti appears in the giant form of the Brahma. This is made of the atoms. It is like this. The power of the Vishnu is infinite, i.e., that is limitless. Being the Almighty Shiva is seated in bhulok on om the earth or he is dominant on the earth.

Reaching here the Almighty eternal Shiva proves benedictory for the making while his bodies name are Shankardeva, Dutt, Satya, Kamgurusha. You desire eagerly even today or earlier for this body and to prove it like this hermits, Yogis and scholar have been involved in penance from their several births with all their experience and inferences form their bodies into Shankar. Question arises here that with the great penance and renunciation of these Yogis, hermits can make this Dev, Dutt, Satya Kam named Purusha with the body of Shankar. No sir, not at all, this is not the answer.

Because the body of Shakar is the eternal Shiva himself in this Kalpa/era. Which have been adorable in the all four eras.

If the god has to incarnate hence he has to propitiate lord Shiva / Shiva Shankar Mahadeva go get his Permission to achieve his aim.

As for example, Ram played the role of the Rameshwar, Krishna assisted Pandavas in the Kurukshetra, so, how can these ordinary hermits, Yogis, saints go beyong that state.

Because the god or 'Kalpeshwar' of this era is the eternal Shiva Mahadeva himself.

Now we come to think here ? if a god incarnates in the human body hence his body is a mortal body or that is perishable or about to end. This is the condition of the Karma Chakra (cycle of Karma) of the nature that one who takes birth, he gets the death but why this Mahakal, Shankar always remain in the form of the eternal Shiva.

18
Enjoyer and Enjoyment

The curiosity remains to till date that whence this god comes viz how it becomes a god. This is just like a physical composition.

The matter of the fact is that only pious or the pure body can be seer. Impure body gets the death.

The Question Arises

Enjoyer and the enjoyment is the father of the birth and death.

Now this eternal Shiva is in meditative posture. Are the enjoyment and enjoyer the condition to transform a Dev, Dutt, Sat, Kam named Purusha into an eternal Shiva.

Yes sir, this proves a condition.

Who is the keeper of this condition ?

For this every form and name (Nama and Rupa) of the Shiva will have to understand. The importance is given to the name and forms of the Shiva and not to the glories.

This is the condition and the examination of the pious body of the Shiva. Why not be it the Shiva, Mahamanava (great human being). Mahakal and the eternal Shiva, this women closure (flame and form-Nana-Rupa) remains under the giant power of lord Vishnu.

19

Darkness : The Death

Now, there is no future of the dark. viz the time has taken all the tree times/tenses the past, present and the future in it sway.

Here, the Mahakal form of Shiva is depending himself from the death in the dark. The master of the giant power Vishnu is permitting Mahakal to be like Shiva or the eternal Shiva. This Vishnu considers Shiva the most loving under his giant power. Therefore, Mahakal in remaining/staying in the heart of giant Vishnu as he is sitting in the dark in the form of the eternal Shiva out of fear from the death.

The prayer to the giant form of Vishnu goes to the Para Brahma the universe or the Brahma.

It seems here that the Yogeshwara giant Vishnu's Yoga is incomplete without the Para Brahma or the Brahma.

This is the last training of Yoga viz it is able. Knowledge of the name/noun is not known

Note : Being a writer this is the pehaps of experience or inference of seven years that what to name the person whow completes Yoga.

Para Brahma is different from the Brahma or the universe.

Narayana is the link to connect the Para Brahma with Brahma. Nara, i.e., water, this is a great element Nara Teja (water + magnificence), i.e., This Nara (water) bears the Agniform after getting its magnificence. This magnificence emanates from Nara which acts like the fire in the air.

This Agni (five) is the form of enjoyment and the enjoyer. Now, the Yoga of this giant Vishnu is waiting for the nomenclature of the Narayana. It will continue till the Yoga Maya Shakti (illusory power of the you) destroys the dark, thus the Narayana remains with the Brahma and the Para Brahma.

Note : While some of the scholars loose both their religion and patience by repeating infinite-infinite, And who- soever practices renunciation, penance and Bhakti, etc., they all get trapped in the cycle of creation and revolve in different species.

Renunciation, penance, Bhakti and Dhama and Karma, etc., are done by the bodies of Dev, Dutt, Satya, Kam Purusha. Now, whatever, this body can do is also the matter lying in between the enjoyment and the enjoyer. The consciousness walks on the inert form Prakriti just like the body runs like a machine.

Now, among these 84 Lakh species whichever's body/ machines is stronger, achieves that type of position. The greatest body or the machine is the human body. When the human body daras to go beyond the limits of the nature or try to go above through his/her conscious power at that time the hunger and the thirst of enjoyment and enjoyer starts burning the machine of the body, hence the soul also starts to run away.

Because body is the both enjoyer and the enjoyment. While the element like Prakriti/nature is also just an inert body which is the part of the giant. The body run by the conscious power is proved by the Deva, Dutt, Sat and Kam.

Thus enjoyment and enjoyer both are regulated by the fire.

Now, the air breath (Vayu pran) which remains separate from the air element and the Prana which is aire element the soul remains with both of these elements. Fire, water-air these two elements emanate from the magnificence.

Virtue of the nature and sexual desire emanating from the

fire of the Brahma matters the soul accompanies the enjoyer and the enjoyment upto that point, where the body wants to go.

Soul can be named but it cannot be proved directly.

This is the chain which links Atma (soul) and Paramatma (god) and for that the scholars, meditating hermits/saints, Yogis keep their bodies heating up birth after birth. That's why the pious body can take birth.

Note : Now the question arises here how this pious body takes birth and how will be that pious body. Piousness and purity make a body Sidha (sear) together. Piousness which comes to the body itself, be pure or be a Sidha (seer) and introducing other Sidha (seers) and the enlightened (Sidhiyan) is the identity of the pure which became pure and Sidha (seen) by becoming chaste.

Now, that is pure, pious, sidha, that is immortal. That is that element which is capable to go beyond the semigod (Adhideva) knowledge. What is the matter to talk about spiritualism. It is extremely difficult to see this element.

Because there is a big difference between the cognitions and the direct proof/evidence. This dilemma can be removed by a Sidha Purusha viz pure and Sidha (seer) body......? That which is proved directly which is the symbol of penancle and cognition.

There is only one place for penance and cognition, at the point and Sudha (seer) body.

That is the Siddha (seer) place which is worshipped by the spiritual people of the mortal world. Such Purusha who are having pure, pious and Sidha bodies are considers pious as long as hey maintain their purity and piousness.

Wisdom in the body lond behind a pure body just like a woman. As the wisdom level increase in the pure body or acts in accordance with the body at that time wisdom starts snatch the thing from the body just like a women who starts snatching all the nights of her husband.

The pure and Siddha body is in danger from the wisdom outside its door and this is just because of respect of the wife, son, grandson, daughter-in-law, husband inside the house and the veiling of the daughter in laws.

As long as the wisdom lags behind, there is the fear that the ego may increase. Ego leads the people fall and lead them to rise above.

The luster of the ego is just like sun which blinds the pure body and pushes it the virtues of the Prakriti and the matters related to the Brahma.

When the human body shines in this luster of virtue of Prakriti and the matters related to Brahma, it mean the body is raised in the ego and its vice-versa is also possible, i.e., if it is immersed/ fallen in the virtue and matters meant it's ego is fallen.

Thus, the pure and Siddha body remains revolving in the virtues of the Prakriti and Matters related to Brahma and the birth and death cycle of the different species. These are just because of wisdom and ego which finished that pure and Siddha body in the ego. And transform that into a barren tand. But where this pure and Siddha body evas worshipped. We have the proof of this even to-day which can be seen. An uncountable number of temple-mosque, church, Gurudwara are lying vacant without its devotees in which no one go and see its conditions. The basic cause of this is that these are the abodes of the virtues of the Prakriti (nature) and the matters related to Brahma and hot related to the Jeeva. Jeeva is the enjoyment of the matters related the Brahma and the virtues of the Prakriti, Jeeva keeps revolving in the cycle of birth and death of the creation in accordance with their Karma. Hence, it is also proved here that enjoyment and the enjoyer is the Jeeva himself. It is just like a candle and its light or the flame. There are just like the symbols of inert and conscious. The flame of the candle keep burning till the candle finishes.

These are not only the symbols of inert and conscious instead a symbol of the pure body or its age.

As long as the body is pure and Siddha (seer), it is the symbol of light of the candle. As long as these inert an conscious are combined, the body of any Yogi, hermit, scholar, meditating person reaming pure, otherwise jeeva in the form of body keeps revolving in the womb, nature (Prakriti) and Brahma in accordance with their – Karma. Soul and the soullessness inert-consious, birth-death. Soul and the soul lessness. Inert- conscious, birth-death, Prakriti and Brahma matters, etc., are the created science of that Almighty alphabet OM Para Brahma Narayana Yogeshwara.

In this era/Kalpa science has made its god. In this era another god/master can not be there. Even if he is a pure or the Siddha body. This era has a god/master that is the Kalpeshwar.

This is the eternal truth of the science of the god. The nomenclature to this Kalpeshwar had to be made that had been made. That nomenclature goes to the eternal Shiva. The eternal Shiva is the Kaleshwar.

The Prakriti (nature) gives as much space to the Kalpeshwara as much is permited by the god.

Similarly, the Kalpeshwara garners as much knowledge and name, little as much is allowed by the god or the ParaBrahma.

As for example the first Purusha, great human being Mahadeva, eternal Shiva. Almighty is proved directly and seated on the creation cycle and appeared in the form of Shankar.

For the creation of this impure and pure creation cycle several took place on this Shankar type body. As for example from Pinda to Anda (from substance to particle), from Anda (particle) to the fire element, from five element to the soul element, etc., appears in the process of examination of the Jyotirlinga and the examination of the soul lessness, the examination of the appearance of the Almighty, passing between the enjoyment and enjoyer, these all have been proved by Purusha of Rajoguna ill usury power (Maya Shakti) Rudrani and to run the creation cyle of the nature.

On account of these examination this type of pure and siddha body was made. Subsequestly Shiva the Almighty appeared from the body to soul and its vice-versa thus becoming the immortal Kalpeshwar.

The matter of the fact is that crossing from all these examinations a pure and Siddha body named Shankar was made.

Wearing red, saffron, yellow cloth the saints, Yogi, hermit started tricking to be a pure and Siddha, Yogi, hermit started tricking to be a pure and Siddha body people are envolved in fulfilling their subsistence in these cloth and long hair, Runciation, penance and meditation are remaining only a word.

Now who can make them Understand

Making or achieving a pious, pure and Siddha a body was beyond the experience and inference of the eternal Shiva, it was the giant Vishnu's grace that he experienced/felt the cognition of the soul-element. Afterwards the eternal Shiva became Gyanendra and be seated in the Pinda from the body was from Pinda to the Anda (particle).

Because of having the first body in this trilateral virtue of the Prakriti or the nature and with universe he became on eternal Shiva, that's why this body Shiva lasts forever. It remaing secure Kalpeshwar in every era.

Here, master of the giant power Vishnu, i.e., Vishnu + atom like devouring the poisonous atoms and kept releasing the water element from his body and subsequent by he immersed or be seated in the water.

This giant supreme Vishnu is bearing every one within himself be it the smaller to the smallest atom or a bigger to the biggest substance like a Jeeva.

The atom which is under the supreme Vishnu that is enjoyment able and the enjoyer.

This able and enjoyer are, in inspite of being mortal, keep evolving.

It is proved here that destruction is the father of evolution.

Now, the god has kept six (6) rights to himself out of these destruction and evolution, viz, birth and death-these two rights have been proved by him. But the secret of birth and death he has kept hidded.

The curiosity to know this secret always create horripilation and let feel a new experience.

It is inherent in the supreme Vishnu viz the atom is within the nature/Prakriti. Is it inert an conscious......? It is enjoyer and enjoyment ?

Does it have any relation with any other element? If it is, what is that element which is the cause of birth and death of the Jeeva and the nature (Prakriti).

Perhaps, this is that element which is the master of both enjoyment and enjoyer. Perhaps, it the matter above the nature/ Prakriti.

The master element of the enjoyment and the enjoyer is its soul.

This is the womder of the science of god-and this science is the proof of the soul.

How does god analyse that great element ? this raises question on the third and fourth right secret, i.e., name and glory of the god. As I have discussed the secret of birth and death earlier just like that the science is the god different from the soul. Whose name and fame are beyond the remembrance power of the manking. The master of the fact is that, it is beyond the capacity of recitation and singing of the words. It is just like a tune or notice.

This is the matter beyond the experience an inference of these scholars, meditaling people, Yogi, hermits saints or philosophers and knower of the self- and every one bends his head in front of that-Leave the laymen the matter of the fact is that four elements/ secrets out of six secrets of the god has been discussed.

20

Birth-death, Name and Glory

Now the atom present in the body of the supreme Vishnu, is there the body of the great human being Mahadeva lying in that or the Vishnu is a great atom or part emanated from the vish + atom or the poisonous atom.

This question highlights the composition of the creation cycle lying in between the Prakriti and the Purusha.

Perhaps these are the virtues emanated from the Vishnu's poisonous creation, i.e., the triple virtue of the Prakriti or nature and the Karma are the particles of poison which do not get destroyed even after the demise of the body. As for example, any body is mortal because of its Karma. But this Shiva-Shankar name body eis so pure and Siddha (seer) that it is equal to the four evas/kalpas, i.e., satyuga, Treta, Dwapar and Kalyuga. This Shiva-Shankar named body is not a mortal one but it is equal to the four yogus or a Kalpa-and it always remains like a Shiv-Shankar that is kalpeshwar or god of the Kalpa. The virtues of the Prakriti and Brahma related matter, are free from the Karma of the creation cycle.

Now, the question arises here that sundry of the saints, Yogis, hermits, knower of the self, Brahma or Bhajna Nandi live and die in the parts of Brahma, Vishnu and Mahesh. Perhaps this is the sway of these supreme powers which tends to the path of Bhakti

These three Devas/duties, Jeeva and body, mind Brahma, wisdom, Vishnu, ego are inherent in the Shiva.

Whatever a body or jeeva does out of his/her mind, wisdom or ego that remains as the matter of the creation. The body or the Jeeva does not go beyond that. Thus the body remains as an enjoyment and enjoyer.

The decision of profit and loss makes a body enjoyer and the enjoyment. Thus the body/Jeeva remains a mortal body. Sexual pleasure becomes the cause of profit and loss. The master of enjoyment and enjoyer, and account of sexual pleasure viz profit and loss make the body of the Jeeva a mortal one or kills that.

These profit and loss are the fifth and sixth periods of the mysticism of the god which are beyond the control of the Jeeva/body because god has kept six rights in his hand. These rights are as follows:-

Birth – death

Name – glory

Profit – loss

The Jeeva or the body keep revolving in these six mysteries. Abode of the body viz Jeeva is th womb, Prakriti/nature and the matters related to Brahma.

There is no Permanent abode for the Body

The claim of the body to be permanent and in the garrison of these six (6) mysteries. But it does not remain permanent.

This is the Shiva named body which become the almighty for ever in the universe. It remain seated in himself for one era/Kalpa because it is a pure, pious and Siddha Shankar's body. Which has been made Kalpeshwar by the entitlement by the god-which is seated like an eternal Shiva.

However, this Shiva-Shankar named body has to be pious, pure through the penance of five element which is both enjoyer and the enjoyment. These are the fundamental element of the grace of the god. It is not in the control of the human being. Such saints, in the guise of a hermit by awakening the fire element of the conscious body, living in a hut or Ashrama with all amenities, bearing four garlands in their neck with very long hair, by Smearing ashes on their body showing their neck as a Yogi and hermit finally ends their life.

Such huts an Ashrams which are lying in a dilapidated state and vacant, their soul keep wandering. Ther proof of this matter is available in different religious.

These wandering souls appears in front of the laymen. Who bassed away before their scheduled time.

Laymen worship those ashram or huts by naming than as a Siddha-Peetha out of their fear and by popularising these Ashram, make a new construction at that place.

Now the question arises here that those who are Yogi-saint or hermit decline and they were pious, pure and Siddha bodies.

Whether it a ordinary public community or religious community or the people belong to any sect or religion. Those who dies their soul keeps wandering and they were not the pious, pure or Siddha Peetha or/bodies.

These orthodox and fearsome people who are the ordinary people keep worshipping those wandering souls by considering their abode as pious, pure and Siddha (seer). This type of people keep constructing such places as religious places out of their faith.

Such orthodox people dissipate orthodoxies through their ill-campaign by recognising those Peer (teacher). Prophet and Moseleum as pure and Siddha. Now, who will make understand such ignorant people that to be a pious, pure and Siddha, the master of the enjoyment and enjoyer-the fire element has to be transparent viz the fire has to emanate from the fire.

After ward the sight of that enlightened, pious, pure and Siddha body and the self is possible. The Shiva has confined the name Shankar from the Pinda to Anda through the penance and deep thinking and enlightenment that is in the form of Pinda or Anda (substance or particle) even to-day. Those are 12 Jyotirlingas.

Enlightening of the self is the philosophy of the element and the self. This is the pure and Siddha Shankar named pious body which is seated in the Linga (fallus) like a dead body or the Shiva and it is enlightened.

From here Formless Brahma is Worshipped in the form of formed Brahma

There are three supreme power. Brahma, Vishnu and Mahesha. However, as the question of the worship of formless Brahma into a formed Brahma was discussed, Hence two powers remained.

Brahma and Para Brahma

Now, let us discuss these two power. Fire is the only element, which gives proofs of the flame or light. This light emanates from the pressure of the air which crosses the water element in the enlightened state. When that Brahma light enlightens. The space element looks infinite. These elements, i.e., water, fire, air, other and the earth are the father of the supreme/giant/eminent Prakriti Brahma but, the Para Brahma is beyond these five elements.

Now, only the power of the Para Brahma remained that is beyond the reach of the Tatva/element.

Now the enjoyment and the enjoyer which are under the control of the fire element, that science is the soul.

This science-soul is called Param Tatva or the Absolute element, that is the science of the god or the Para Brahma.

At the house of God, the path ot the Para Brahma ends.

That is the ParaBrahma Paramatma, one Tat Sat which is called a house of god.

The body which is pure and Siddha reaches at the door of the house of the god where Dev, Dutt, Sat, Kam named Purusha reside. It is just like this......

Dev-The pure part of the god, soul......that is

Dutt-The god should be just like a sacrificial altar in which offering are poured just like the food is poured in the mouth. Thus the god should be pious like Dutt.

Sat-That which can not go against the soul element or the self and that comes along with the eternal truth.

Kam-That who works religiously/that who does his Karma (sexual pleasure) religioiusly, hence the Artha tends to salvation. The person should be a workaolic/ a Karmayogi.

Nama-The name, which is named by the god/devoted god, that does not differentiate between male and the female, that should be based on the help of the god.

Purusha-A soul that should be pure and blotless. That is neither male nor female, that should be only the particle of the science of the god. That Almighty god is the Purusha. That is known like this, Supreme god is the Purusha. That is known like this.

In such a pure and the Siddha body, the alphabet OM Para Brahma Paramatma is its OM Tat Sat.

That Para Brahma is the only power/entity which is above the Brahma.

Now, the entity which is in side power of the Brahma, that gets trapped in the name and the word. Whatever that is Jeeva, virtue, matter, word, name, etc., all be silent through saying only Ahm Brahm Ashm!

Now this alphabet OM Para Brahma Almighty god Narayana Nara + Ayan/ion (the water element) has come out from the water element as a result of Proclamation of the fire element which was pressurised by the air element. That element Tatvam Vidheyak Atma/soul element clashes with the element and gets finished. This soul has no body in fact the other element has no limit form or it is infinite which give birth to infinite space/ universe. This is the master of Bhooh Bhavah Svah (भू; भव: स्व:), i.e., the supreme god.

That who is born, named and prepares characters himself and establishes religioin that does not remain the master, even if being the master of the people/world (Lok) legitimately because of on the basis of people of characters, he gets the nomenclature of the gods.

On account of separation he acquires the possessed form of the Brahma and becomes god. Therefore, it is proved by this that alphabet OM Para Brahma Parmatma being the security of all the Bhootas/elements provides the character of the god. Therefore that is the god.

Thus the formless Brahma is worshipped the possessed form of the Brahma. These are direct proofs.

Now we should discuss the Para Brahma god or the supreme god that why this alphabet OM is the Para Brahma Paramatma or the supreme god.

As is the soulessness/Anatma from element to element, Jeeva in the nature, in the creation cycle, the "science of soul" always remains in equal properties with all the souless beings, birth and deat, name and glory profit and loss.

That is the Karma or the witness and the science of the God is Soul

This is a great mystery that being the part of god, separated and the regulator of the creation cycle in the grcat/giant Prakriti and the Brahma, being the separate/private security of all the souless being, he is the "beholder of the creation" as well as the creator of vision/panorma.

This is the particle of light of expressed-inexpressed, dead/ mortal-nectar, mastery of the knowledge.

God is the Knowledge of all Sciences in Himself

That is different in every one, he is different from others himself.

Therefore, that alphabet OM Para Brahma Paramatma (or the supreme god) Narayana being the Yoga of everyone is a Yogeshwara. This is the matter to be understood. This is three from three is equal to three, two from two is equal to two and one from one is equal to one that is a part of void (zero) and from void to inexpressed. This is the OM Bhoor Bhoovah Swah (ॐ भूः भूवः स्वः) and that is swah Bhoov Bhoor (स्वः भूवः भूः) is OM!

That Para Brahma/god is the master of the existence of the alphabet OM.

Despite knowing like this, the world/people seeks proof or the curious one should say "I am the Para Brahma".

Now, how can I say the world/people that I am that alphabet Om Para Brahma Paramatma Yogeshwara. This is the path which tends to salvation, this is the Yoga path of the alphabet Om Para Brahma Paramatma Narayana Yogeshwara which tends to his house-ek Dham.

That is A House of God

At last, emphasis has been given on mind and thinking which are inevitable to keep the body pure.

Now, let us think. Thinking happens with the mind or the garland-this does not make any difference. Whether thinking happens with the mind or with the garland or with other means, these all are the matter after the entry into the Brahma. Brahma is the word, thinking and mind, the matters related to the Brahma are through the words. This is the matter of the tradition/decorum that you are born from which individual, thing or the place.

This Depends on the Power of the Birth and the Birth Place

Now, you may have the knowledge that just after taking the birth one think-Ahm Brahma is etc.

"I am Brahma, is the only word. This word 'I' will purge my body.

Therefore, the first thinking done by the mind is for the word "I" (self) the subsequently, whatever thinking will be done by the mind, will depend on the tradition or the decorum.

Now how have the decorums met but the power which make use to enter into the Brahma is the conscious power/consciousness. Which keeps the Jeeva or the body into infinite species in the existence of Brahma. This conscious power is the amazing creation of the supreme god/Parabrahma or it can be said the science of the god in which all knowledge is inherent/hidden.

Therefore. We will have to Understand the Consciousness/Conscious Power First

Now, the person who has pure mind and birth-place, he will have the pure body, if the body is pure, the mind will be pure, if the mind is pure, the thinking will be pure and if this much is pure, the thinking will be pure and if this much is pure, hence the Yogi, saint-hermit, scholar-meditating person will garrison you for your examination. In this garrison, all the effects of the matters related to the Brahma in the Prakriti and the conscious power/consciousness of the Para Brahma will attack on your pure body, for example, in a garland there are 108 gems and that garland in your neck is the insignia of your thinking. Because every gem of the garland is the symbol of the thinking.

Every gem of the garland is he symbol of knowledge. Every scholar/gyani has written an Upanished. The great seers/saints have written 108 Puranas. The Vedas are the speeches of the Brahma. At loss Shree mad Bhaga want declared itself the supreme, viz, if it become the symbol of the supreme knowledge and stands out in knowledge and stands out in front of the and raises a question, hence I feel trapped.

The composition of this starategy has garrisoned me from all the rounds with round chain of their hands. There are ready to extinguish or finish my consciousness.

I am trying to search out an alternative to break these barriers where-

I am seeing the greatest barrier of these 108 Upanisads. My second barrier is 18 Puranas

I am seeing the four Vedas as my third barrier. And the last barrier is the one Shree Mahabhagawat which is posing my challenge.

Ahm Brahma Asmi (अइं ब्रह्म अस्मि)

I am the Brahma

On account of facing so much knowledge and powers, my mind, thinking and the conscious power begins to shout- "I am the Brahma". (अहम् ब्रह्म अस्मि)

Because this conscious power is the achievement of god which is stronger than the body. This is the wonder of science of the Para Brahma.

Like this......When the consciousness exhibits power in the body, hence all the sensory organs become restless. With the help

of wisdom, mind wants self satisfaction. When self-satisfaction is not their, hence on individual feels constained for argument, the constrained mind causes individual weak and ill. Ths weakness of the human being makes him silent.

Now argument in the silence is the thinking/pondering.

This thinking, which is an argument within the mind, these Upanishads, Purshas, Vedas, Shree Madabhegawat, matters related to Brahma, the power of the nature the giant are feeling restless to bring those in the Verbal arguments.

Restless to bring their trilateral power into existence. The giant/supreme says, "you say, I am Brahma".

S.K. Parashar

Note : Second Edition of this book to be Released soon.

I said me ?.......I am different from you and me.

The supreme said, so you are not with me.

I said......I am with one. I do not live with two.

The supreme said......who is that one ?

I said......this Brahma and the Para Brahma is the one.

Therefore, I am also one.

The supreme said-These all are in me. Whole universe is

I said- you are inherent in all three. I am a Para Brahma.

The supreme said- what is the Brahma ?

I said......I am the Brahma

The supreme said......what is the Para Brahma ?

I said......The alternative of my thinking by my mind is the Para Brahma.

The supreme said......who I am ?

I said......you are everything. I am nothing.

Hence the supreme said- amen (तथास्तु)

I kept watching, the supreme disappeared and I reached to my thinking. I have finished this Ist volume here. You, please wait for the 2nd volume.

At least, I present this poem to the changing time/period of nowadays.....

The pauper wants to give up his poverty and says.....

Neither give excessive misery nor give excessive happiness.

O giver, please do not give poverty to anyone.

Correction of rich is here

The life of every poor is a waste here

Kinds of thou travels in car

Separate schools are built]

Naked leg drenched with the dust

With hunger they are those paupers
Do they make history,
When their body is clothless
Why did you give the birth earlier, why did you give this remorse
If you have given the happiness, never give even shadow of remorse.
......o, give, never give poverty to anyone......
Seating like a ma'Om
Smears cream and powder.
Car, disco, dance liking
Come with liquor drinking.
Mother and sisters in the noble family
Sheds their sweat and blood
Keeping clothless their body
Extinguishes the fire of their stomach
Be someone crying, be someone laughing,
Never give such intoxicated fragrance......
O, giver never give poverty to anyone
Crying child in the lap
This is ornament of the poor
Mother, unable to see hungry
Beholders are in sundry
There is no name of mercy-responsibility/Dhrama
There is no love in anyone's heart.
World becomes dark in carnal desire
How is this world......

What was named, what work was given,
Never give these satan the mercy (Habibi)......
O, give, never give poverty to anyone......
No respect for the poor
Gold the respect for the poor
Thus the poverty got victimised
This is the matter of crying.
Sitting with their full of god own
This is gold without bread.
Corruption prevalent here.
Life has to be lost here.
When this garb remain, how this country will last.
Never give nearness to the subordination......
O, giver, please, never give poverty to anyone.

S.K. Parashar